SACRED

JOURNEY

MEDICINE BEAR PUBLISHING
BLUE HILL, MAINE
USA

SACRED ——— JOURNEY

ESSENTIAL TEACHINGS FOR THE DAWN OF A NEW AGE

*Channeled Messages
from the Ascended Masters
and Selected Writings*

by

ERIC KLEIN

MEDICINE BEAR PUBLISHING
BLUE HILL, MAINE
USA

SACRED JOURNEY: ESSENTIAL TEACHINGS FOR THE
DAWN OF A NEW AGE

© 1998 by Eric Klein
Published 1998.

02 01 00 99 98   0 9 8 7 6 5 4 3 2 1

══════════════════

COVER ILLUSTRATION BY SHAWN MONROE

EDITING, TYPOGRAPHY & DESIGN BY
SARA BENJAMIN-RHODES
(CELESTIAL COOPERATIVES)

══════════════════

ISBN 1-891850-08-3

Library of Congress Catalog Card Number 98-87475

Printed in USA on acid-free paper

MEDICINE BEAR PUBLISHING
P.O. BOX 1075
BLUE HILL, ME 04614-1075
USA

CONTENTS

CONTENTS

Dedication

To Maharaj Ji, to Sananda, to Amma Chi, to the Self in All.

Acknowledgements

Grateful thanks to Sara Benjamin-Rhodes for editing, type-setting, and for her persistent dedication to this work; to Marie Damschen for many selfless hours and years of transcribing the channelings; to Shawn Monroe for the cover art; to Scott Bach, Reindjen Anselmi, Phyllis Hamilton, and to Barbara Berger and her sons for their loyal friendship and support; and to Christine, always, for her love.

FOREWORD
(How this book was born)

Having published four books of channelings in four years, I honestly felt I had completed the channel/author phase of my life and was looking forward with anticipation to returning to my long-cherished anonymity. My philosophy has always been to "say what you came to say and get off the stage."

Then, in 1997, a Swiss publisher commissioned me to write an article about the spiritual path to be published in German translation. Just as I was completing the article ("The Spiral Path"), she asked me if I would make it much longer and talk about my personal experiences with the Ascended Masters. Before she made this request, I had thought about recording my personal story, but my inherent resistance to the work involved had always precluded me from starting the project. Though writing has been my occupation for some years, it is still not something I undertake willingly (with the notable exception of song lyrics!).

Coincidentally (?), at this time I was experiencing some rather difficult health problems, to the point that the mortality of my physical body was becoming a much more immediate possibility. It seemed that if I were going to share the story of my life's journey with family, friends, and loyal readers, I had better not waste any more time! The plain, straightforward style of the *Sacred Journey* narrative attests to my mental state at that time. I was simply trying to finish the job with as little embellishment and as much honesty as possible.

While concluding this expanded article, I was inspired to add a closing channeling by Sananda to complete the package. While speaking on the phone to my transcriptionist (whose selfless work has filled the pages of most of my books), she told me that as we were speaking, Sananda was repeatedly reminding her about one of the channelings we had transcribed from the "Ocean of Love" classes, my last public work as a channel. Grateful for the "helpful hint" from above, I dug out the transcriptions, which I had forgotten about with the passage of time. By the time I had read far enough to find the message Sananda was referring us to, I was quite intoxicated! The channelings were wonderful, almost certainly the purest and vibrationally highest of all those that I had experienced over the years. At that point, there was no doubt that these messages should be included and that this sometimes lazy author had been tricked into writing one more book.

In retrospect, I can only say how grateful I am to have been given the opportunity to complete the cycle of my channeled books with these powerful and loving messages from the Masters who have supported this work for so long. I pray that in these pages you will find the inspiration and support you need on your own sacred journey. I am honored to have been used in this small way for the benefit of my fellow devotees of Truth. May all sentient beings benefit!

Eric Klein
Santa Cruz, California
May 1998

Part One

THE SPIRAL PATH

Steps and Stages of the Spiritual Path

*W*ithin each human being, in the core of our hearts, resides an essential longing. It is an ever-present desire to return to our true home, the God-Presence, the Self of Selves, the Source. This innate longing of the soul is the force that propels us through all of our human incarnations, as we slowly but steadily climb the evolutionary ladder into higher states of existence.

Ancient Indian scriptures often refer to the human body as the "Crown of Creation," for it is both a mortal, physical manifestation and a mystical doorway into spiritual immortality. The Upanishads state that the human soul is the "Bridge Between Time and Eternity." It is our ability to cross this bridge through the divine gift of Self-awareness, that lifts us from a merely natural, animalistic existence into supernatural union with the infinite, omnipresent Source.

It is only after an extensive journey through every aspect of material existence, over many lifetimes, that a human being begins to open to a deeper awareness of the true purpose and meaning of life. The subtle presence of the spiritual Self, long overshadowed in our headstrong rush to absorb worldly experiences, begins to assert itself in our lives. We begin to hear its persistent call from within for a return to our true home in the Real. The acknowledgement of this inner call and the inevitable decline of interest in the fascinations of purely material pursuits mark the initial stage of the spiritual path.

STEPS & STAGES OF THE SPIRITUAL PATH

The Ascended Masters have stated many times that there is only one spiritual path, and that we are all on it. This statement reflects a vast perspective that embraces the evolutionary progress of all sentient beings in many dimensions of physical and non-physical existence. For the purposes of this article (and because of my own necessarily limited human perspective), I will narrow my focus to address the spiritual path as I have personally experienced it: first from within a fairly traditional "Eastern" view, and then later on from a "New Age" frame of reference. I will attempt to somewhat artificially separate the path into six distinct stages or phases of personal growth. These delineations can be useful to our understanding, but know that, in reality, they are only labels. Each human being will pass through these phases of experience in their own unique way, following their own unique timetable. So, for the purpose of this limited discussion only, I will use the following descriptive titles to represent the characteristic stages of the path: The Seeker, The Aspirant, The Initiate, The Devotee (or Disciple), The Master, and The Ascended Master.

The Seeker ⸺

The seeker has heard the call of the spiritual inner Self and has heeded that call. He has opened himself to the awareness of an invisible higher power, mysterious but real, and is taking steps to search for a deeper understanding of existence. The seeker is like a detective, looking for clues that will help him to solve the mystery of life. Using both intellect and intuition, he follows the trail of this mystery, leaving no clue unexamined.

The way of the seeker leads through many varied experiences. In his search for the way to a deeper contact with the mystery of the Divine, he will often read assorted scriptures and spiritual books. He will sift and sort through teachings, old and new, looking for the path that is right for him. Often he will feel drawn to attend religious or metaphysical gatherings, sampling from the many teachings and practices available.

Often confused by the apparent discrepancies between these teachings, the seeker must persevere, using his own "common sense" and intuition to find a spiritual path he feels confident can take him farther along in his attempt to solve the great mystery. Finally, in response to his sincere efforts, and at the perfect time, a distinct teacher or path will appear that sufficiently addresses his needs and concerns, a teaching that both satisfies his intellect and that resonates in the heart as Truth.

The Aspirant —

Following the search for a compatible teaching or path, the seeker stands at the doorway with humility and sincerity, requesting acceptance and training. He has become an aspirant, aspiring to receive the teachings or initiations offered by that path. At this point, he has realized the need for direct assistance if he is ever to proceed beyond a merely intellectual understanding into a real experience of the Divine. His heart and soul call from within, beckoning him to go deeper into the mystery, and he responds by committing to a more serious study and practice.

Each unique spiritual path will have its own "doorway," its own method of accepting new aspirants. Most physical Masters require that a period of sincere study and spiritual practice be demonstrated by new aspirants who wish to be accepted. On less traditional paths, especially those without the physical presence of a living Master, this process is informal and primarily internal to the student. Nevertheless, there is always a "doorway" to enter and an attitude of dedication required before the aspirant is offered the blessings and responsibilities of walking the spiritual path in earnest.

The Initiate —

Once the aspirant has demonstrated his sincerity and dedication, the spiritual Master accepts him as a student. This acceptance, or initiation, can be a formal ceremony or an informal gesture by the Master. But whatever the case, this initiation is not merely symbolic. It is a profound opening of the Master to receive the new student, and begins the deep commitment of the Master to the initiate's spiritual progress. At this point, the Master assumes responsibility for the spiritual development of the student, requiring in exchange only a commitment to follow the teachings and practices of the path. A true living Master, or Satguru, is capable of taking on and transmuting much of the initiate's negative karma (the cumulative total of positive and negative energy created by our actions in previous lifetimes, which must be balanced before Self-Realization can occur), thereby dramatically quickening the student's progress toward Union with the Self.

Whether a particular path is traditional or (like many of the New Age paths) more metaphysical, a human being cannot pass into or beyond the stage of the initiate without the blessing and assistance of a Self-Realized Master in physical or non-physical (Ascended) form. Whether we are aware of their presence or not, the Satgurus and Ascended Masters have been guiding our evolutionary progress since this "Earth School" began.

The Devotee —

After initiation, the longest and most intensive phase of the path to Self-Realization begins. The earlier stages can be passed through very quickly, especially by those who have followed the spiritual path in previous lifetimes. But the continuation of the journey demands that the initiate make spiritual practice their first priority in life. The Devotee must be in tune with the inner Self to the degree that following the direction of his Teachers takes precedence over mundane pursuits. This does not imply an irresponsible attitude toward worldly commitments but, from this point onward, spiritual practice quite naturally becomes the essential focus.

And true devotion is required if a student is to acquire the "homeward momentum" required to sustain him through the often intense growth processes to come. For in this phase of the path, all ego-centered activities and attachments must be offered up on the altar of the Higher Self. Here the devotee will experience the profound love and protection of the Master and of his invisible Guides, as well as the primal force of the ego's resistance to its own dissolution. For it is truly necessary that the limited ego identity be "swallowed up" in union with the infinite Self before we can be fully awakened to who and what we are.

The illusory veils projected by the ego mind are all that separate us from the experience of the immortal Self. The devotee is shown many glimpses of this ultimate Self as he continues his practice. At times the veils are seen to be insubstantial as clouds, while at other times the devotee will feel tightly bound by the cords of illusion, even to the point of despair. It is only the grace and protection of the Masters that carry us through these incredible transformations. Ultimately, devotion is a gift, and one that is far beyond our ability to repay. It is a precious gift that must be nurtured in the heart. It is only our acceptance and surrender to this gift of devotion that transforms our mundane lives into a magical love affair with the eternal Self.

Before continuing through to the conclusion of this discussion of the stages of the spiritual path, I feel it important to give the reader some insight into my own process as I attempt to communicate these often subtle concepts. In the previous segments, I have been able to speak directly from my own personal experience. I have not yet, however, completed the attainment of the following stages: The Master and the Ascended Master. So, while the experience of 25 years of meditation and study with several living Masters (and of ten years of channeling the Ascended Masters) may qualify me to speak about these advanced states of awareness, it does not give me the ability to speak directly *from* these states of awareness — an important distinction. I will simply do the best I can, and apologize for any inconsistencies caused by my own limitations.

The Master —

While the devotee may have experienced many deep insights and spiritual transformations, he has not yet completed the path. Only in that moment when complete and permanent union with the Self is achieved does the devotee graduate into Mastery. This mystical union, referred to by many names (Enlightenment, God-Realization, Self-Realization, and Cosmic Consciousness, among others) is the attainment of a permanent and effortless state of oneness with the God-Self. All of the well-known spiritual teachers (such as Jesus, Buddha and Krishna) and numerous lesser-known Masters have operated from this state of awareness. Beings in this state of God-Consciousness are filled with the infinite love and bliss of the Divine, having finally and completely transcended the limited ego identity. The Master has achieved liberation from the effects of karma and is forever free from the continual rounds of birth, death and re-birth experienced by mortal human beings. The individual goal of the spiritual path on Earth has been completed.

But what is a being, having achieved this liberation, to do from this point on? Having transcended any individual desires, the Master turns his full attention to teaching and assisting other human beings. This selfless activity can take many forms, and each Master seems to manifest unique aspects of the Divine. Whatever their form of service, each Realized Master acts as an open window into the infinite, blessing and advancing all souls fortunate enough to come into their presence.

The Ascended Master ⸻

Though the attainment of Self-Realization may mark the successful completion of the spiritual path on Earth, it is only the climax of the physical phase of the journey. Growth and evolution continue as the spirit gradually proceeds through ever higher and more spiritual dimensions of existence. The first dramatic step into these higher dimensions is the Ascension.

When the soul's training on Earth is completed in Mastery, and when the Master's world service is concluded, the Self-Realized human is given an opportunity to finally and completely transcend the physical realm by taking on an exclusively spiritual form of existence. In Buddhist terminology, this new form is called the "Rainbow Body." In New Age circles, it is usually referred to as the "Light Body." This mystical transformation marks the conclusion of the soul's voyage through time and space, for the Ascended Masters are no longer bound by the constraints of these lower dimensions of existence. They are free, immortal, spiritual beings, who exist only to serve as guides and healers to all evolving entities.

The Ascended Masters have the ability to project their love and healing energies to human beings who are sufficiently open to receive them. They can transmit spiritual Grace and communicate telepathic guidance in answer to our prayers. They have the ability to materialize a visible body on Earth for brief periods of time (if required by a mission of service) and to de-materialize instantly when their task is completed. They are true Masters of time and space, whose infinite love simply must be experienced to be appreciated. Above all, the Ascended Masters serve as examples of what is possible for all human beings to one day achieve.

⟜ THE SPIRITUAL HIERARCHY ⟞

I would like to proceed as quickly as possible, following this general discussion of the stages of the spiritual path, to areas that I feel much more capable of speaking about: my own personal experiences with the Masters. But first I am feeling guided to speak a bit about some of the many spiritual entities interacting with us and with our world at this critical point in our evolutionary cycle. Again, my understanding of these spiritual beings is far from complete, so I will apologize in advance, to them and to you, for my own limitations.

Invisible Visitors —

The universe is a vast, multi-dimensional creation, inhabited by entities existing in the third (physical) dimension and also by innumerable beings existing in more spiritual forms (the fourth dimension and beyond). Our physical senses are capable only of receiving information from third-dimensional sources. This is why most humans cannot "see" Angels, Ascended Masters or any of the other spiritual beings that surround us.

Spiritual practice can, over time, awaken our dormant "spiritual senses," allowing us to occasionally "see" or "hear" or "feel" the presence of these higher-dimensional beings. These types of experiences are not the purpose of personal growth, of course, but they are quite often a by-product of our process of awakening. Conscious encounters with these invisible entities can be extremely beneficial, since they can share wonderful healing energies and divine inspiration with those of us preparing to "graduate" from the physical classroom of the Earth school. These encounters can also be rather disconcerting, if one is not first prepared by some years of spiritual practice. For this reason, I am including the following general information and some brief advice on inter-dimensional etiquette.

The Fourth Dimension —

Described in the simplest terms, the fourth dimension occupies the vibrational frequency ranges immediately beyond our physical reality. This includes the realms humans commonly refer to as the Heavens and the Hells, where human souls are sent after the death of the physical body. Fourth-dimensional beings are non-physical, but not immortal. They are learning from their various states of pleasure or pain in preparation for their next human birth, their next opportunity to achieve liberation from the wheel of birth and death through spiritual growth.

Some fourth-dimensional beings can act as guides to souls in transition between physical life and death. Some can share information with psychic explorers, though this information is often limited, as many fourth-dimensional beings are just as lost and confused as most physical humans. My practice has been to avoid contact with fourth-dimensional entities altogether, by requesting (prior to meditation and channeling) that I experience only beings from the fifth dimension or higher, the abode of the Angels and Ascended Masters.

The Fifth Dimension and Beyond —

Through my meditations and channeling I have been blessed with countless beautiful interactions with Ascended

Masters and Angelic guides. But still, from my limited human perspective, it is impossible to accurately determine the various dimensions or higher states of existence from which these blissful encounters originate. I can only honestly say that there is a Spiritual Hierarchy of immortal beings existing in many higher dimensions and serving a Divine Plan. I cannot say whether Sananda (Jesus), or Buddha, or Mother Mary, or Archangel Michael operate from the same dimension, nor do I feel that this kind of rational analysis is even pertinent to descriptions of spiritual phenomenon so far beyond our human conception.

What can be said, without any doubt, is that these higher-dimensional beings are working together in harmony and for our benefit. The supreme intention behind this divinely orchestrated effort is nothing less than the awakening and spiritual advancement of all sentient beings in all inter-dimensional corners of the universe! The Creative Source, the Universal Self, offers its infinite Love and assistance through these numerous messengers. Beings at each dimension of existence are "reaching back" to help lift those below them onto the next step on the spiral stair of evolution.

The Ascended Masters —

The term Ascended Master refers most specifically to those beings who have walked on Earth as humans and successfully graduated into the Ascended State as a result of their completion of the spiritual path. The majority of the Masters I have worked with in channelings fall into this category, and I believe it is their own unique experiences as humans that allow them to understand and assist our process so appropriately. Some of these Masters have been known under different names in different cultures and contexts, so I thought it might be helpful to include a partial listing of some of these teachers, along with some of their more well-known Earth lifetimes. Why the Masters choose to contact channels under various names is, I believe, an appreciation of the individual limitations within the belief systems of those of us who are attempting to channel them. In my experience, Sananda (Jesus) will respond just as effectively to those addressing him by his Earth name (Jesus) as to those using his lesser known cosmic name (Sananda). I refer to him as Sananda simply because when I asked him which name I should use, in the context of our teaching and channeling work, that was his response.

At any rate, the following is a partial list of the Ascended Masters I have had personal contact with, and in parenthesis (when known), some of the lifetimes they are said to have lived on Earth prior to their Ascension. The name currently used by the Ascended Master is often, but not always, similar to the name used in their last human lifetime.

Sananda (Jesus)

Saint Germain (The Hebrew prophet Samuel, St. Joseph, Merlin, Christopher Columbus, Le Comte de St. Germain)

Kuthumi (Thutmose III, Pythagoras, St. Francis of Assisi, Koot Hoomi Lal Singh)

Serapis Bey (Atlantean High Priest, Amenhotep III)

El Morya (King Arthur, El Morya Khan)

Also: Buddha, Krishna, Baba Ji, Meher Baba, Kuan Yin, Ananda Moyi Ma

Extraterrestrial Visitors ⟞

In relating to extraterrestrial beings, I suggest the same guidelines as used with all other invisible visitors. Request of your inner Self and your Guides that you encounter only beings from the fifth dimension or higher, and then only if it is highest wisdom for your evolutionary growth.

Because the Earth is such an extraordinary world, and because our world is preparing to make a profound evolutionary leap (called by many "The New Age"), we have attracted a multitude of guests from throughout the universe. Some of these are physical beings like ourselves, and many others are Masters in their own right, here in service and cooperating closely with the more familiar Ascended Masters and Angels.

I have personally experienced one group of extraterrestrial Masters who are quite active and closely aligned with Sananda. They have been referred to in New Age circles simply as "The Confederation" or as "The Ashtar Command," after one who communicates through myself and others as Commander Ashtar. This powerful, benevolent Master has shared wonderful transformational energy, along with information about our planet's evolutionary process. About Ashtar and his associates, I can definitely say that they serve the Divine Plan with love and compassion, guiding our world in its re-birth as a member of the cosmic family.

On Channeling ──

Receiving spiritual awakenings and inspiration through channeling can be extremely beneficial. To feel the presence of the Ascended Masters and Angels is always a blissful experience, a glimpse of the higher states of awareness that await us on the path. But discernment is always required when exploring this phenomenon.

The Masters have often said that there are no 100% perfect channels on Earth. And in fact, there are many more channels in the New Age arena who are far less accurate or "pure." A pure channeling is one in which the participants can really feel the loving, healing presence of the Ascended Masters. The purest channel is one who has been prepared by long study and spiritual practice, and who has no motive other then to surrender to Spirit for the upliftment of all.

The highest manifestation of channeling involves the participants in the same manner that devotees sit in the presence of their physical Master, basking in the Guru's radiance and healing grace. To participate in channeling from a merely intellectual perspective, to receive "cosmic information" or psychic predictions, is not the most beneficial motivation. In fact, all channeled information should be verified by the discerning organ of the listener's heart. Our own inner guidance must always take precedence over information received from external sources.

My suggestion is that all seekers place powerful tools like prayer, meditation and service first and foremost in your spiritual practice, allowing the heart's inner guidance to lead you to the perfect Teachers (living or ascended) for you. If it is highest wisdom that you serve as a channel for the Ascended Masters, they will contact you at the perfect moment. Ultimately, all phenomena — including channeling — will be transcended as we approach our ultimate goal: Self-Realization.

Belief And Truth —

Beliefs are common to all human beings, but no two human beings share identical beliefs. What we believe is based upon our own relative experiences and on the input we have absorbed from external sources. It is human nature to have preconceptions and to form misconceptions about spiritual matters.

The spiritual seeker must learn to recognize the essential separation between the beliefs of the mind and Truth. Truth is the primordial energy, the eternal foundation of all existence. Truth can only be experienced as a result of a spiritual practice that lifts our perception beyond the mind into oneness with the infinite. Truth cannot be spoken in language. It is the Self itself, known only through the experience of Union. It is what we become.

Part Two

SACRED JOURNEY

My Journey So Far

*M*any people have asked me to speak about my own spiritual path, and especially about my experiences with the Ascended Masters. In response, I offer this brief history of my personal journey in the hope that it may benefit those whose hearts are now calling them to embark on their own spiritual quest. Know that you are not alone.

Seeker, Aspirant, Initiate

I was born in 1951 in the city of Cleveland, Ohio. My childhood was normal and quite unremarkable, as I learned quite early to hide my artistic and spiritual tendencies — qualities that were definitely not valued in my middle class home and schools. It was not until my late teens that the inner longing for a more creative, less materialistic life began to assert itself.

The first truly spiritual awakenings came during my college years, when I began to experience spontaneous *satori* states of consciousness while alone in nature or walking around the school grounds. (Satori is a Zen Buddhist term. A satori experience is a sudden awakening, a powerful glimpse through the veils of mundane reality into the essential, spiritual foundation of awareness. These experiences are extremely blissful and transforming, but are usually brief in duration.) What I was shown during these powerful experiences was a pure and stunning beauty, a promise that there was something profound in this life that was real and well worth searching for.

During the next two years I sought out and read books on Eastern religions, mainly Buddhism, and tried to re-create my Satori experiences using various meditation techniques. Though largely unsuccessful, my efforts and the readings did give me a basic understanding of the fundamental principals of the spiritual path. They also helped me to articulate a goal that would help to give meaning and direction to my life. I'll never forget the look of shock on my Eastern Religion professor's face when, in a private consultation, I told him that I had made the attainment of Enlightenment my life's goal. Apparently, I was not meant to take the study of the Buddha's teachings quite so seriously!

By my third year of college, I had come to the decision to drop out of school and begin my spiritual path in earnest. My vague plan was to hitchhike west to the Rocky Mountains in search of a place where I could live simply and meditate. While the initial preparations for my journey were underway, I saw a poster advertising an appearance by an Indian devotee of a spiritual teacher, Satguru Maharaj Ji. I went to the meeting and sat in rapt attention as an elderly man in saffron robes (called a Mahatma, or Great Soul) told the story of his own search for Enlightenment. Finally, here was someone speaking my language! After his discourse, to my delight and amazement, he announced that the following morning there would be an initiation for those sincerely interested.

That next day, in March of 1972, affected my life perhaps more than any other, for it was there that I was blessed to receive my initiation in the ancient art of meditation. The Mahatma, after hours of discourse and preparation, selected a small group of us that he felt were ready to receive the initiation. Then, after having the lights dimmed, he touched each of us on the forehead, opening the third eye *chakra* to reveal the Inner Light. As we sat in speechless, somewhat disoriented bliss, he taught us how to meditate on this Inner Light, as well as several other simple meditation techniques. He told us that these same techniques had been taught by Jesus, Buddha, Krishna and innumerable other Satgurus through the ages. I felt as if, after having been lost for years in the wasteland, I had stumbled onto the road to paradise.

Devotee Years —

Having been miraculously spared the necessity of my planned western journey, several other initiates and I were guided to form an Ashram, a place where we could live together and be supported in our spiritual practice. It was during the next two years, while living there and in several other spiritual communities, that I began to understand the real requirements of the path I had chosen. I especially began to understand and appreciate the role played by the Guru, without whose energetic assistance my spiritual practice would have continued to be fruitless. I realized that no matter how much effort I applied to meditation practice, it was only when my effort was enhanced by the grace of a Self-Realized Master that I was lifted into a real experience of the divine Inner Self.

In 1974, circumstances in my personal life, along with the persistent inner longing for a deeper contact with the Self, forced me to take an honest look at myself and my level of dedication to the path. Painfully, I had to acknowledge that my spiritual practice, though consistent, had not been sincere enough to take me into the higher states of consciousness I knew existed behind the veils of ego-centered thoughts and projections. I saw that I was going through the motions of a devotee, without the inner fire of devotion needed to break through into real communion with the Self. Compassion for all sentient beings was understood as a concept, but was not yet a living reality in my heart.

At this turning point, I began an intense but beautiful period of meditation, fasting and Satsang (the sharing of spiritual discourse with devotees and other seekers) that resulted in many powerful breakthroughs. Where I had been meditating for one or two hours per day, I now began sitting for four to six hours, diving deeply into the waves of bliss that come from within when illusory thoughts and ego projections are silenced.

At this time, spiritual practice became my entire focus. Worldly pursuits held no attraction. In search of a warmer climate where we could live outdoors like simple yogis, a close companion and I migrated southward, camping as we went. After months of fasting and meditation, we found ourselves in the campground of a National Forest in central Florida. It was in that strange forest of oak and palm trees that I received my first experience of the Enlightenment I had been seeking.

Tired and weak from fasting, I felt at the very end of my energy. In a moment of utter surrender, I realized that I would not be able to continue living that way any longer. The path of asceticism had left me physically and emotionally exhausted. Sitting down on a blanket of fallen oak leaves, I offered myself one last time in prayer to God and to my Guru. In total resignation to whatever fate held in store, I said that I had only the strength for one more meditation, for one more attempt at Realization, before I would have to give up this crazy path forever.

In the next moment, completely by the power of Grace, I was given an experience that would forever change my perception of life. I was shown Enlightenment. I was granted a deep and extended experience of the true underlying Reality. In that one moment, my perception somehow pierced the veils of illusion. I recognized the Oneness of all things. I laughed at the sheer folly of spiritual practices that attempt to take us to a place we have never really left. I understood how pleasure and pain are identical. I was taken to where there never was an "I" and never would be. There was only one Self, always. All sentient beings were already Home. Returning to lie down in my tent, I received my first telepathic message: "From now on your meditations will not be for yourself but for the world."

This experience, at the same time both cosmic and utterly normal, opened me in some way I have never been able to describe. It was as if an inner door had opened inside me into an immense, conscious void beyond time and space. From that time on, that same healing energy poured through me whenever I began to speak about the spiritual path. In retrospect, I now see that this is where my "channeling" experiences really began.

The "Real" World —

From that point on, the life of a wandering ascetic became not only unnecessary, but humorously absurd. Though I tried for a time to live in a tent in the green Appalachian hills outside Athens, Ohio, I found myself drawn more and more to the company of other devotees. In a matter of several weeks I was living in town, and within that year I had fallen in love and gotten married. Within another year I was the father of twins! Without a doubt, the truest test of my spirituality was just beginning.

The next seven years, from 1976 to 1983, were a challenging balancing act. Between the demands of parenthood and work I found little time to indulge in my usual extended meditations. It was a period filled with both the grace and blessings of our Guru, Maharaj Ji, and with the wearying demands of the material world. The most profound blessing at this time was the healing, heart-opening presence of my children. It was through my playful interactions with them that I learned some of the most valuable lessons about what a truly spiritual life is. The material world may ultimately be an illusion in time, but to really live the spiritual path requires us to honor the Creator's dream by living as impeccably as we can, doing the work that is before us in each moment.

The Quest Continues —

In 1984 I was in a fragile state, brought on by the stress of divorce and by seven draining years in a soul-deadening government job. I was forced to acknowledge that a major change was needed. Just at this time, at a small party of friends, I was surprised with the news that my ex-wife and her new husband were planning to move to the state of Florida, taking the children with them. As is always the case, difficult times provide the greatest opportunities for growth. After coming to terms with the emotional trauma of this separation, I recognized that a new doorway was opening in my life, and resolved to walk through it into whatever fate held in store.

Later that year, a girlfriend and I sold most of our possessions, bought a used van, and left Ohio on a journey we called "The Spiritual Quest." We headed west, with no plan but to follow our intuition, and after several months and many adventures finally settled in Santa Cruz, California, a well-known mecca for artists and spiritual seekers. It was here, while searching for a spiritual community, that I attended my first channeling sessions and felt the door to an unimagined future open a step farther.

Etheric Retreats —

Exposure to channelings of the Ascended Masters had a powerful and instantaneous effect on me. For some time, my own meditations had been less than satisfying. My internal connection with Maharaj Ji seemed to have been mysteriously severed, a difficult adjustment for me after so many years as a disciple. But now, these blissful encounters, with Ascended Masters Baba Ji and Meher Baba, again inspired me and satisfied my need for real contact with the God-Presence within. I drank deeply and gratefully from this newly discovered oasis in the midst of the desert of materialism.

From then on, whenever I sat to meditate I would pray first to request the presence and grace of the Ascended Masters. I began to experience beautiful interactions, at first entirely non-verbal, with invisible beings who would surround me with love and peace and healing energy. As I became more open and trusting, I was taken on wonderful inner journeys, often to an etheric retreat I came to call "The Cave of Five."

These magical journeys always began with a deep meditation, within which I would feel my spiritual body spontaneously separate from my physical body and rise upwards, flying through etheric clouds of energy and light. I then would "touch down" on a flat rocky ledge on a mountain in what felt like the Himalayas, where I would find myself standing at the open entrance of a cave carved out of the rock. Entering the cave, I would find five robed Masters sitting in meditation. On my first visit, their leader signaled me towards him and introduced himself as "Tulku" (a title I later learned refers to a specific type of Tibetan Buddhist spiritual teacher). He asked me to sit down and meditate before the Masters, and as I did this they began to send powerful rays of healing and purifying energy through my body. When this blissful process was complete, I bowed in gratitude, walked out of the cave and, in just the way I had come, was transported back to my body, still sitting in its usual meditation spot. I was completely unaware of how long (in Earth time) I had been gone. I also had no idea that this would be just one of many incredible etheric journeys, beyond time and space, yet to come.

On one of the most remarkable of these journeys, Tulku called me to the back wall of the cave and pushed open a stone door. It opened, not into another room, but into boundless space. As I stood staring in utter amazement at distant stars and a nearby planetary system, he unceremoniously pushed me out of the door! Instantly, I found myself simultaneously experiencing intense fear and the delightful feeling of free-falling through space. As joy and excitement overcame my fear, I realized I was "flying" towards a nearby, Earth-like planet, whose surface was penetrated at intervals by narrow columns of light extending many miles up through the atmosphere. I "landed" at the base of one of these light vortexes, in a desert canyon with walls of red rock, and was met there by three more Masters in the form of Native American shamans. They gently guided me to sit neck-deep in a pit of liquid mud, and began singing a repeating, three-octave healing chant. As they sang, I felt my chakras (the seven major spiritual energy centers in the human body) opening and balancing in a series of deeply relaxing energy waves.

After some time in the mud pit, the singing gradually died away and then stopped. The shamans then lifted me out, washed me off with water, and led me to stand on a wide, table-like rock surface. The leader of the three shamans directed me to stand perfectly still, and to maintain my balance by fixing my concentration exclusively on the soles of my feet, no matter what transpired. As he backed away, the energy vortex descended around me and began to spin. Standing in the eye of the vortex, I fought fear and disorientation, knowing somehow that if I did not maintain my focus as directed I would fly off in a thousand energetic fragments. I held my concentration for as long as I could, feeling the powerful purifying force of the spinning vortex, but finally I was overcome by the intensity. Just as I began to feel myself slipping off into some unknown dimension, the spinning stopped and the shamans carried me down, congratulating me on my successful completion of the "grounding ceremony."

I returned from this strange experience in a wonderful state, feeling as if every cell in my body had been activated and purified. I felt blissful, calm, balanced, open and fearless. Though my mind had no frame of reference from which to understand these etheric adventures, the benefits to my spiritual growth and well-being were undeniable.

Inner Voices —

My meditations and inner adventures continued, with many more trips to the Cave of Five and other etheric settings. The results of these experiences were always profoundly uplifting, but at the same time I felt a longing to channel the healing energy and messages of the Masters in a way that others could experience as well. In my prayers, I began to ask the Ascended Masters — if it was highest wisdom — to come and speak through me in the way I had experienced in the channeling sessions, not only for myself, but for the benefit of all. I felt the need to try to share these wonderful energetic transformations.

One evening, while meditating in my bedroom, I received an answer to my prayers. I began to feel the presence of a gentle energy around me, and the sensation of a higher consciousness merging with my own. Just at the moment when I began to feel I might be able to "channel" this being, my girlfriend spontaneously walked in and sat down in front of me. I began to hear a subtle inner voice, slowly repeating simple words and phrases, pausing after each phrase so that I could repeat it aloud. Gradually overcoming my initial doubt and resistance, I began to repeat the words I was hearing, whispering quietly for fear of breaking the spell. The messages were simple and tender, bearing with them a love that was intoxicating. After a few minutes the presence withdrew, and to my delight another took its place within me, speaking in the same slow patient way, sharing an equally loving, but subtly different energy.

This first channeling experience ended after three Ascended Masters had spoken: Saint Germain, Mother Mary, and Sananda (Jesus). My girlfriend and I were ecstatic, feeling we had been blessed to receive a sacred and mysterious gift.

Further Initiations ——

The floodgates were now open, and I began to channel the Masters at every opportunity. We gathered regularly with several other beginners to practice, with wonderful results. At first the messages were quite simple, interspersed with many silent pauses, as we grew accustomed to the process. But within a few months my girlfriend and I were proficient enough to channel together whenever we wished. The Masters supported our initial efforts with a compassionate patience that was a powerful lesson in itself.

Many invisible guests began to introduce themselves, some we knew and some we had never heard of before. Different Masters would come each time I sat to meditate, each sharing their own unique energies and opening me to receive ever more powerful transmissions. In a typical session, Saint Germain might come first, opening my third eye to receive intense infusions of light, helping to improve my receptivity to telepathic messages. Then he would withdraw and Baba Ji might come, politely introducing himself and working on the throat center to help heal my fear of self-expression. Finally, El Morya might come to work on the third chakra, empowering me by grounding the spiritual energies more deeply into my physical body. These training sessions went on for many months, dramatically improving my channeling ability and teaching me to easily distinguish the subtle energetic differences between each Master. In a short time, I was able to instantly identify the presence of each Master by their characteristic energetic signatures.

One morning, Ananda Moyi Ma, a female Master who had lived in India early in this century (as a God-intoxicated incarnation of the Divine Mother) introduced herself with a powerful wave of love and bliss. She told me that the Masters had a gift they had been holding for me for just that time. I was immediately drawn deeply into a *samadhi* (a timeless state of blissful union with the Self) so strong that my mind and body seemed to dissolve into a pure consciousness of all-permeating love. The scent of roses filled the room, intoxicating me, though there were no flowers anywhere in the house. The experience lasted for two or three hours, but I was beyond time, and would have remained in that state forever had I been allowed to. Words simply cannot describe the immeasurable Love that exists within us.

Twin Flames ⸻

Throughout the next year, I continued to study with and channel dozens of Masters, but from the beginning Saint Germain had become the most regular channeled guest. He became my main teacher and guided me gently through my inner and outer life. One day I received a phone call from a woman who had been advised by another channeller to come to me in order to receive a personal message from Saint Germain. We made an appointment for a private session and met a week later.

Her name was Christine, and from our first meeting we felt an indescribable spiritual connection. In the channeling Saint Germain surprised us by suggesting that we spend more time together, and we began to meet weekly to exchange my channeling for her acupuncture treatments. Although I was already in a relationship, I felt strongly attracted to this warm and sincere seeker. It was not an ordinary sexual attraction, but something occurring deep in my soul. I soon discovered that she also felt this same mysterious attraction. Within a few months — with the prompting of Saint Germain, our invisible matchmaker — I ended my previous relationship and Christine and I were together. He told us that we were twin flames, and that our union was vital to our happiness as well as to our spiritual growth.

This is the simplified picture the Masters used in describing to us the Twin Flame phenomenon: A soul is created like a solar flare bursting forth from the surface of the Godhead, the Great Central Sun. In that moment, the individual flare separates into masculine and feminine polarities, into two twin flames. These two souls proceed individually along their evolutionary paths through many embodiments, meeting occasionally as human beings. It is a beautiful and blessed event when finally, after ages of growth and experience, these twin flames meet and recognize one another.

The Masters have said many times that the reunion of twin flames is a natural result of many lifetimes of spiritual practice and evolution. I can only say, from my own human perspective, that without the love and healing presence of Christine in my life, I would never have had the strength to follow the guidance of the Masters through all the confronting challenges of the work that was to come. In a lifetime of blessings, this is one I am continually thankful for.

Two years after our meeting, in July of 1990, Christine and I were married in a small ceremony at Panther Meadow on the slopes of Mt. Shasta. Appropriately, the guest of honor was Saint Germain, who spoke through our channeling minister and held us all spellbound within his gentle grace.

A New Teacher —

Over the next year (1988) the training sessions continued, most often with Christine, who was herself beginning to channel. We worked with many Masters, but Saint Germain continued to be our main teacher, and we came to rely more and more on his intimate presence and guidance. It was a magical time, with many visits to our favorite retreat, Mt. Shasta.

In the spring of 1989, we took a longer trip to Sedona, Arizona, to experience for ourselves the many spiritual energy vortexes said to exist there. One afternoon we climbed high up onto Bell Rock, one of the most well known vortex sites, and sat on a stone ledge to meditate and channel the Masters. We received only one brief message, but it was one that confused and saddened us. Saint Germain told us that the work we had been doing was complete, and that we would no longer be spending so much time together. I, especially, had come to depend on his continual presence and direction, and felt lost and abandoned.

But soon, in the following weeks, a new Master appeared, descending in a powerfully focused ray of light to continue our training. His name was Ashtar, and about himself he would say only that he was an extraterrestrial Master here to assist us in our growth. He proved to be completely familiar with the Masters we had been working with, including Saint Germain, and said he would be continuing with more intensive training in preparation for our work in the world. We gladly gave ourselves to this new course of study, which continued to include visits from the other Masters as well, including an occasional session with our beloved Saint Germain. Over this time we came to understand much more about the Masters and the way in which they coordinate their teaching work, and soon came to love and appreciate our mysterious new friend as much as any of our older teachers.

Earthquake ——

By the autumn of 1989, I had been working full time for several years as a production manager for a fast-growing garment manufacturing company. It was a stressful environment, and I was praying intensely for a new direction. I was hoping to be able to somehow earn my living in a way that was more in alignment with my spiritual path. One afternoon, my life did take a new direction, and in a much more dramatic fashion than I could ever have anticipated. At 5 p.m. on October 17, 1989, the Loma Prieta Earthquake struck, devastating our town and shaking me out of my familiar office into an uncertain new life. Many of the buildings in the Santa Cruz area were destroyed, including the plant where most of our production was done. Fortunately, there were few injuries from the earthquake, but strangely, within thirty seconds my job had become obsolete.

Guidance and Trust ——

As we were recovering from the trauma of the quake, and after most of the strong aftershocks had passed, it was time to go within and seek guidance about how to proceed. The new freedom offered by my sudden unemployment was both exhilarating and frightening, and I put all of my previous training to work in extended meditation sessions, requesting direction from the Masters.

One cold evening, while meditating in a rocking chair in front of the wood stove, I felt an extraordinary energy descend around me. It was Sananda (Jesus), whom I recognized from our previous channeling sessions. But this time the sensation of his powerful presence was many times stronger than ever before. My mind and body became totally still, almost paralyzed, as I felt our energies uniting both spiritually and on what felt like a cellular level. The sensation was of another completely distinct body, invisible but as solid as my own, merging with mine. The love and bliss were overpowering. Though my mind was completely stilled and full of light, it felt crystal clear and receptive. In this sacred moment, Sananda told me that he would be teaching through me for the remainder of my life on Earth.

The powerful reality of this experience was undeniable. In that moment I did not know or care what form this teaching would take. The mere fact of Sananda's intense, intimate love brought forth a flood of gratitude and tears.

A short time after this, one of Christine's acupuncture patients learned that I was channeling Ashtar and brought us several books about him. I had no idea that anyone but us had ever heard of this Master, and was eager to read his messages presented through other channels. It was through these books (by Tuella and Ariana Sheran) that I was first introduced to the alliance of extraterrestrial Masters referred to as the "Ashtar Command," and to information about their role in the fulfillment of the Divine Plan for Planet Earth. Much of what I read was familiar, but some of the information concerning "Light Ships" and their involvement in the "Planetary Ascension process" was both new and all but unbelievable.

Basically, these messages stated that within our lifetimes the Earth would undergo radical physical and spiritual transformations, and that there were likely to be mass ascensions in which many thousands or millions of humans would attain a higher-dimensional level of existence previously known only by the Ascended Masters. This complete transformation and purification of the Earth and of all human beings was to mark the beginning of a New Age of peace and harmony, a total spiritual rebirth. Though in later research I would find very similar predictions in the Bible, the Koran, and in many Native American prophecies, at that time these ideas were new to me.

My first reaction was to try to contact Ashtar myself, to ask him to comment on the accuracy of this information. He came through immediately, and said that while no channeling is 100% accurate, in general this information was true. In this same powerful channeling he also asked me, to my shock and surprise, if I would be willing to teach a course on it! As Ashtar withdrew, several more Masters, including Sananda, came through to volunteer their enthusiastic support of this new Ascension Course. I was beginning to feel like the victim of a divine conspiracy!

Public Work ———

For six months prior to the earthquake, I had been hosting a weekly meditation and channeling in our home, with a regular group of ten to fifteen people. Each week a different Master would bring through an intimate and spontaneous discourse about the spiritual path, usually concluding with a brief group meditation and energetic healing. To channel in this way had become quite natural for me, but the prospect of the Ascended Masters publicly teaching a formal course through me — and one based on this outrageous new information so far beyond my personal experience or my ability to verify — was, to say the least, frightening.

Nevertheless, in many powerful and reassuring personal sessions, the compassionate support of the Masters, along with Christine's encouragement, soon helped me to surrender to the process. The Masters promised that they would take charge of the classes, and that any personal doubts about my readiness for such an undertaking were unfounded. They said that I had been well prepared for this work over many years, and that I would soon understand why they had invested so much love and patience in my training.

So, in February of 1990, after six weeks of intensive inner preparation, in which the Masters presented me with an outline of the course and a personal preview of Sananda's discourse for class number one, the first of the six weekly Ascension Classes* began. The Masters (Sananda, Ashtar, Saint Germain, and Archangel Michael) proved true to their promise, and came through with such power and focus that I had only to let go and allow them to work their energetic magic. Prior to each class, the Master involved would give me a preview of his discourse and a profound experience of his presence, so that I would be as open as possible to the higher frequencies of spiritual energy they were to transmit. The energies that flowed through me at this time were extremely blissful, but they also stretched me beyond anything I had experienced before. My life was feeling more and more like surfing a tidal wave of Spirit. I know it was only the power of Grace that held me up and kept me from being overwhelmed.

The Ascension Classes were received with such enthusiasm that, in order to accommodate the demand by new students, it became necessary to repeat the series three times between February and August of 1990. Cassette tapes of the classes began circulating, first in the U.S. and later in England and Australia. To my surprise, I began to receive scores of letters and phone calls from around the world, from people wanting to learn more. It really was astonishing to me that these channelings, given to a small class of twenty people in my own living room, were inspiring such a response.

A Spiritual Family —

During and after the Ascension Classes, the regular weekly channelings continued, attracting new students and supporting

---

* These channelings, and all the public channelings after that time were recorded and are available on cassette tape. To obtain a catalog of available titles, see the contact information on page 144.

the ongoing practice of the previous graduates. In early autumn, I began to receive invitations from groups in other cities and towns to come and channel. In response to these requests, the Masters created an outline for a two-day retreat they titled a "Starseed Activation Workshop." ("Starseed" is a term often used to describe a soul from a higher dimension of evolution that voluntarily embodies as a human being on Earth to enhance their own spiritual evolution through service. "Lightworker" is a similar New Age expression, meaning generally the same thing.) The Masters encouraged the two of us to accept these opportunities, and so began two rather intense years of travel, teaching, and spiritual adventures.

To our surprise, in the course of these travels we discovered that we were not alone, but part of a large network of Starseeds scattered throughout the world. Everywhere we went, we were met by a small but enthusiastic group that felt immediately familiar to us. We realized that we were part of a family of Lightworkers whose general Earth mission was to assist the upliftment of the entire planetary consciousness, a mission that required us to begin by first awakening ourselves from our own forgetful slumbers! In powerfully transforming group sessions, we witnessed the Ascended Masters opening the Lightworkers to their true spiritual natures and activating them in their functions as emissaries of the divine. Quite often, after one of these powerful weekends, we would learn that some of the participants had begun to channel the Masters or experience other spiritual awakenings.

Although the traveling and long channeling sessions were very draining for my physical body, my spirit was soaring to new heights, empowering me to overcome temporary hardships for the sake of a higher goal. Christine's healing abilities were regularly put to the test, helping my already delicate system to survive the illness I always experienced after flying. Many times I prayed for the attainment of the Ascension, not only to better serve humanity, but also so I could experience the benefits of instantaneous inter-dimensional travel!

Glimpses of the Past —

My foremost difficulty during the course of this intense period of teaching and channeling was the recurring feeling that I was unworthy or incompetent to do the work I had been given. I could not fathom why the Masters had chosen me rather than a more advanced spiritual teacher to be the channel for their messages. Many times I wanted to retire back into comfortable anonymity to avoid confronting my fears of public teaching.

The method used by the Masters to help me overcome these fears and self-limiting beliefs was brilliant. They helped me to recognize the source of these feelings by revealing detailed glimpses of several of my previous lives on Earth. I was allowed to briefly, but vividly, re-experience portions of my lives in Atlantis, in the Anasazi period in the American Southwest, and in my life with Jesus, among others. The common thread running through all of these past lives was that in coming forward as a teacher or prophet, I had either been killed or had failed to achieve the desired acceptance of my message. These experiences had programmed me to view public exposure as a life-threatening occurrence, and one to be avoided.

These fascinating revelations definitely helped me to understand the source of my irrational fears, and showed me that the service I had been guided to perform was merely a natural continuation of the work I had done many times before. Over time I learned to be less attached to my own limited, pre-conceived notions about the results of the work in favor of simply enjoying the moment to moment process. The spiritual path definitely requires an attitude of surrender, of letting go, especially as we find ourselves performing service in the world.

Report to the Command —

In 1991, approximately one year after the original Ascension Classes, I was blessed with what has probably been my most profound and surprising experience with the Ascended Masters. One morning, while sitting in meditation, I was taken on another etheric journey. I felt my consciousness being lifted rapidly upward, through what appeared to be energetic clouds or layers of light. Moving rapidly through many levels of increasingly higher spiritual vibration, I passed through a large portal into what I somehow immediately recognized as one of the huge, inter-dimensional light ships of the Ashtar Command.

I found myself, in an etheric body, standing in what appeared to be a large council chamber. Before me was an oval-shaped table, around which were seated approximately twenty members of the Command. I instinctively took the only empty chair, noticing to my right side the brilliant forms of Ashtar and Sananda. It is almost impossible to describe my sense of detached fascination. Like a silent witness, I felt my normal consciousness observing and making its usual mental notes, but these perceptions were separate, having no effect on the actions of my etheric self sitting at the table.

Just as I was beginning to wonder what I was doing in such exalted company, Sananda shocked me by turning and asking me if I was ready to make my report! Much to the surprise of my silent observer self, I watched my etheric self stand and prepare to speak to the group. In what was a truly strange and fascinating experience, in a process exactly the opposite of my earthly channelings, I listened as my Higher Self channeled the words of my worldly self for the collected Masters. What I heard was a clear and moving account of the experience of the Starseeds on Earth, told from an entirely human perspective, and the extreme difficulties we have experienced in our many lifetimes of service on this planet.

The report, received attentively and sometimes tearfully by the members of the Command, focused finally on the apparently limited success our efforts have had in the uplifting of human consciousness over thousands of years. To my astonishment, as I concluded my report, Sananda turned again and asked what course of action I would recommend! My response was immediate and (to myself, at least) predictable. I suggested that the Starseeds be immediately evacuated from the planet, to be returned to the higher spiritual dimensions from which we had come. Sananda then turned to the council and asked the members of the Command for their reaction to my proposal. The majority of the Commanders raised their hands, signifying their agreement. Finally, Sananda thanked me for my report and told me he would report back soon with his decision.

Within minutes, in just the way I had come, I was gently returned to my physical body in its usual meditation seat, where I sat in total amazement for some time. Somewhat disoriented, it took time for the reality of this incredible experience to sink in through my normal awareness. It seemed both utterly fantastic and somehow entirely normal. In a supreme state of bliss, with tears of joy and gratitude, I thanked Sananda and the Masters for allowing me such an opportunity. Perhaps this was the first time I truly and completely accepted the reality of the presence of the Ashtar Command and of the many channeled messages I had received.

Two days later, in my morning meditation, Sananda again filled me with his light and presence, saying that he was honoring his promise to report back with the results of his deliberations and with the guidance he himself had received from higher sources. He said that it would not be highest wisdom to immediately evacuate the Starseeds from the surface of the Earth, as this would be detrimental to the Divine Plan. He said that this course of action was indeed possible, but that it would abandon humanity and close the door to those preparing to make the shift into higher consciousness. He asked that we, as Lightworkers, continue for a short time more to pursue the completion of our mission, with compassion and trust. He said that although our desire for ascension or evacuation could not be immediately fulfilled, he would initiate a "new dispensation" of love and support for all humans on the ascension path — a ray of love from his heart to ours — that would make our last days on Earth more joyful and more connected to Source. He said that this dispensation would greatly accelerate our growth and our ability to manifest positive results in our spiritual work.

The Masters Withdraw —

The next several years, from 1992 through 1995, were filled with many more wonderful personal experiences and public channelings. Four books containing the most important of these channelings were published, and along with the tape recordings, found their way into the hands of awakening Lightworkers around the world. Many other channels contacted me as well, often to say that they had received messages very similar to my own. It was inspiring to hear the many stories of awakenings that had occurred to people while listening to the tapes. And it was, as always, humbling to witness the Ascended Masters at work, allowing me a small part in their divine play.

Gradually, during this time, the nature of my relationship with the Masters began to change. Where previously they had been quite active in my training, they now began to step back and allow me to put that training into practice. Though they continued to surround me with their grace and presence, and to transmit their healing messages in the public channeling sessions, in my day-to-day meditation practice I was no longer receiving the constant personal guidance I had become so accustomed to. As all true Masters do, they continued to support me without interfering with the sacred process of my own Self-Realization.

At first I was confused by this change and felt abandoned, as I had before when my relationship with Maharaj Ji had begun to change and when Saint Germain had stepped back to allow Ashtar and then Sananda to act as my main teachers. But slowly I recognized that I was in a new phase of the path, and tried to let go of my attachment to the old ways while continuing to meditate and pray for guidance from within. And this guidance did come, though not always in the form of channeled messages. Now I was beginning to feel directed more through my own developing intuition, through a direct sense of "knowingness." Somehow I would just know how to proceed, without any formal messages from external guides. The Ascended Masters did continue to occasionally share personal messages in my meditations, supporting my growth process with loving encouragement, but for the most part they simply refused to tell me what to do any longer.

Realized Souls —

The spiritual path is always a powerful lesson in synchronicity. Just as I was adjusting to this difficult transition with the Ascended Masters, I was blessed with further teachings that helped me to understand and appreciate the valuable lessons I was receiving. Many of these lessons came directly through the guidance of my own inner Self, and many were inspired by my interactions with two unique physical Masters who entered my life at the perfect moment.

The first of these new teachers was Deva Pratyusha (Praty), a woman originally from California who, like myself, had spent many years on the spiritual path under the guidance of her own Indian guru. Praty and her husband had lived for several years at the guru's ashram in India, and then spent eleven more years practicing in seclusion in New Zealand. It was during this intensive period of spiritual practice in New Zealand that Praty awakened into Self-Realization. Soon after returning to California she was guided to move to Santa Cruz, where we magically met and began our work together.

It is a rare blessing when one comes into contact with a Self-Realized soul, and an even greater blessing to be fortunate enough to spend long periods of time in close personal interaction. For me, coming when it did, just as I was feeling uncertain of my path, this was a strong affirmation that we do receive the assistance we require at every stage of our growth.

Praty and I had many private sessions together, each of us sharing our personal experiences and many extraordinary infusions of Divine Grace. Some months later we taught a course together that we called the "Ocean of Love." It combined the channeled messages of the Ascended Masters with Praty's practical guidance and inspiring personal example. But the greatest blessing for me was to receive feedback from one who had succeeded in achieving the spiritual goal I had set for myself so many years earlier. Praty helped me to understand much more clearly the relationship between the inner Self and the physical and Ascended Masters I had studied with so long. She understood the spiritual path, especially the later stages, in which the devotee must undergo the deepest and most confronting transformations. She helped me to see that my own doubts and fears were the inescapable result of the death of the ego prior to the re-birth in the Self. The reassurance that I was proceeding normally and naturally along the path was an invaluable gift, and one that can only be shared by one who has already passed through the fire.

The most remarkable of these two new Teachers is Mata Amritanandamayi (Amma Chi), an Indian Avatar and living incarnation of the Divine Mother. I learned of her through some of Christine's friends who had visited the U.S. ashram in California during one of her annual world tours. On Amma Chi's next visit, Christine went to see her and received Darshan (the spiritual blessing received when in the physical presence of a Satguru). The effects of this Darshan were so profound that I also was inspired to open myself to this new Master, and soon found myself at her feet.

It is difficult to explain the powerful effect Amma Chi had on us. The physical presence of a Divine Incarnation is truly a mystery beyond my ability to comprehend. It is something that simply must be experienced to be appreciated. I can only say that Amma came into our lives like a wind from Heaven, healing our hearts and intensifying our devotion to Spirit as profoundly as any Master, living or Ascended, had ever done before. In daily Darshan sessions she gently hugs each visitor, healing with the all-accepting love of the Universal Mother. Those moments in her Divine embrace, or falling deeply into her eyes, the eyes of the Self itself, are a revelation of indescribable beauty and compassion.

Amma Chi's presence comes to me often in my meditations, or in response to my prayers, in just the same gentle yet powerful way that Sananda or the other Ascended Masters had come to me. Her Divine expression as a physical Master has taught me not to limit Spirit to any one form of manifestation, but to remain always open to receive the next initiation in whatever way it comes. Ultimately, all true teachings direct us back to the God-Presence within. All true Masters, living or Ascended, exist in union with that one omnipresent Self, reflecting that same Self through their own unique personalities. Inevitably, with their assistance, we will all do the same.

On Retreat —

Walking the spiritual path requires one to be dedicated to following the direction of Spirit in each moment. Following that guidance, whether received as a message from physical or Ascended Masters or through the intuitive direction of the inner Self, becomes the primary focus of one's life. Our devotion to the Self is our sanctuary through the difficult passages we all must face in our human existence. Beyond a certain point on the path, we must follow that inner call (no matter what external judgment we might face) with trust and humility.

In this spirit, late in 1995 I felt guided to take an extended break from public channeling and teaching. Although there was disappointment among some who had become overly dependent upon the regular sessions with the Ascended Masters, for me this was an invaluable opportunity to retreat into a more peaceful life, for the integration of the previous teachings and for the healing of my physical body, which had definitely been overtaxed by so many powerful channelings. Trust has been the underlying theme of this most recent period of my life, as I have often wondered how I would be able to support myself without the income from the public work. But the Self has provided, often quite magically, for both my material and spiritual needs, teaching me to surrender to my own childlike dependence on the power of Grace. Through health and financial challenges, I have come to realize more deeply than ever that it is always only this power of Divine Grace that sustains us and all life in each moment. For a devotee of the infinite Self, every challenge is ultimately transformed into a blessing.

To this very moment, the only real home I have after the fading illusions of past and future dreams, life continues as an increasingly magical journey back to Source. In my daily prayers I continue to ask for the assistance of Amma Chi and the Ascended Masters, requesting liberation through Self-Realization and that the blessings of each meditation might go forth for the benefit of all sentient beings. I offer the days of my life to the Self, and pray that my personal limitations will not intrude upon whatever future service I am called on to perform. I look to see the same Self within all beings, each of us a uniquely individual mask of God. I give thanks for the blessings of the Masters, and for the blessings of my tears. And I thank each of you here in this moment, for all that you will become on your own sacred journeys.

I leave you with these lyrics from one of my songs...

Mystic Traveler

I am a lonesome traveler,
A creature of the miles.
I've made my way in solitude,
In my own ragged style.

I've chased the secrets 'cross the Earth,
The mountains and the seas.
I've fallen and I've gotten up,
Stumbling into ecstasy.

I climbed a tower made of light,
To see what Heaven sees.
Where the angels in their flight
Stopped a while and spoke to me.

Acquainted with the underworld,
T'was there, after I fell,
I rode upon the devil's back
Through all the provinces of Hell.

The worlds I've seen
And kingdoms green
All rise and fall
Inside a dream,
Inside a dream.

I sat in council with the sun,
Upon the shores of time,
Drinking in the poetry
He poured out like golden wine.

But don't let my rhymes trouble you;
Take comfort in your days.
I'll soon be passing like the wind,
And you'll forget all that I say.

The ages turn;
We cry to learn.
The divine flame
Inside us burns.

When Buddha was a traveler
With just a begging bowl,
No one could ever beg or steal
What he'd discovered in his soul.

The wheel turns;
We die to learn.
The divine flame
Inside us burns,
Inside us burns.

Part Three

THE OCEAN OF LOVE

Messages from the Ascended Masters

THE OCEAN OF LOVE

Mother Mary

*M*y beloveds, this is Mother Mary here with you. I would like to welcome you to this wonderful exploration of the Ocean of Love. I would like to invite you to relax yourselves and be at home. There are many divine energies and Masters working with you. Many more will work with you throughout this course. We have indeed had a hand in inspiring the creation of this course, and we on our side of the divine curtain are extremely happy that this promise is now coming into manifestation for you and, indeed, as a blessing for this entire planet. For the energies that come through this vortex of love and light, passing through your gathering, truly will flow to all sentient beings of Earth, and especially into the hearts of those who are now awakening, especially into the hearts of those who are just beginning to question the meaning and purpose of existence. So many are asking the deeper questions: "What is the path? Where is happiness? Where is joy? Where is that feeling of love that I felt at one time in my life? Is it possible to know God the Creator, the Divine Presence? Is it possible to have my questions answered? Is there something more to this life, to this existence, than birth and death over and over again?"

You see, my dear ones, at this time the Grace is flowing so strongly. The questions are being answered. Every opening in each heart is being filled with light. You are ones who have already committed yourselves to the spiritual path. Whether you define it as your path to personal growth and empowerment, whether you define it as the spiritual path to God-Realization, or whether you think of it in terms of the Ascension Path, there is but one path, and all beings in all worlds of creation are upon it. If you think you're not on it, you are mistaken. If you think its something that you can fall off of or do wrong and be punished with separation, again you are wrong. Each moment of your lives has been a perfectly orchestrated pathway to this very moment that we share, and to this great awakening that is now manifesting. I would like to honor each of you for your commitment, for having the awareness and the receptivity to be with us in this way. We will be working on many levels energetically, with love and light and healing. We will be working to clarify questions, to illuminate the path a bit more for you so that you can recognize that indeed you are on it, and indeed it is your true direction. We will be working this day specifically to reconnect you with that longing that exists within you to return to your Source. So these energies will be coming through as subtle, or perhaps not so subtle, activations for you. You will feel within you different emotions, or energies, or experiences rising as a result of our transmissions from the higher dimensions. You will be also experiencing a lifting and healing of obstacles, your personal karmic tendencies, the habit patterns that keep you in the illusion of separation. So in the course of our classes, and our channelings specifically, we will be activating you in various ways to inspire within you a longing for that which is now possible — not a longing for that which is a dream, but the longing and the desire and the devotion that will definitely manifest in your return home, practically, in a real way.

The Ocean of Love is another way of describing the God-Presence within all that exists. The Ocean of Love is simply the essential energetic component within all creation. At the very source and center of your beings, of every being in all dimensions and all universes, this Love is present, this nurturing Divine Essence. In your spiritual practice, you can feel the waves of this Ocean of Love breaking within your souls, within your beings. Throughout all manifested existence, throughout all embodiments and within each moment of your trials and challenges here on this Earth, these waves of Divine Love have been crashing within you. To live without contact with the Ocean of Love is sorrow. To feel it only occasionally in your life, only rarely, is a deeper sorrow, for you recognize it and then it is gone. You who have committed yourselves to the spiritual path have the courage to pass through those phases that are difficult, for you have felt this Love. And yet it is not always at your command in a practical way that you can feel. That is why at times beings on the spiritual path may sense a feeling of regret: "Well, I was happy when I was making a lot of money and working at the bank and sailing on my yacht. I was relatively happy. Then this spiritual awakening occurred and I recognized a deeper happiness that made my limited happiness seem pale and shallow in comparison." And in that moment, after your honeymoon with God, there is often the opportunity for despair to creep in, to feel that, "Well, now I know of the existence of this divinity, this beautiful presence. And yet, where is it when I need it?" What we will be working on, dear ones, is to prepare you to move through that phase of the spiritual path into Union, so that the fulfillment of the promise that was made to you the first time that you felt the Divine Love within you will be realized.

I will be here throughout this course and throughout your lives, and I will be offering my energetic healings to you. I am one of your hosts, or I should say, your hostess. So again, I thank you for having the courage to follow your inspiration to be here with us, for having the courage to come face to face with your very existence, and to be totally honest with yourselves about where you are. Where you are perhaps feeling disconnected or empty, offer that up for healing and I will be with you. I am your Divine Mother, and I offer myself to you. When you are feeling the need for more love, for more nurturing, call upon me. Just ask. Go within, relax yourselves, and feel my presence within you. So it is time for me to go. Sananda would like to speak with you.

THE INNER FLAME

Sananda

*G*reetings my divine guinea pigs! I hope you are enjoying our experiment so far. This is Sananda. You will be hearing from me often in the course of our gatherings, along with other Masters who have been specifically directed to work to open you to the Ocean of Love within you. It is time now. The preliminaries are over. It is time for the main event in your lives. All beings who are now active on the spiritual path are feeling an energetic call within their hearts. It is a call from the very depths, from the very center of the soul, you could say. It is the call of the Real. It is a call that tells you that there are magical events about to occur within your consciousness in a very personal way, in a very real way, regardless of what external phenomenon you may be witnessing in this world.

No matter what phenomenon that may be fascinating you, there is the Real, there is the longing within you to return to Union. Human beings on this world come into existence in a very open and sensitive state. They have within their bodies, as small children, as babies, very simple needs: the need for love, the need to feel connected with Source. As you are all divine children of your Mother/Father God, you have within you that simple, childlike need to feel the presence, to merge with the presence of the Mother/Father energies that you are. In your training in this world you are taught very quickly that this inner longing is something to be suppressed, that it cannot possibly be fulfilled. You are taught to try to fill that vacuum within your heart with careers and relationships, with many fascinations and phenomena. And very quickly beings forget that they even have within their hearts this unresolved yearning. And yet it exists. It is unquenched, no matter how many lifetimes a being has existed and given themselves to illusion, to separation. At the very core, at the very center of the soul, exists a flame that will not die.

Ordinarily, human beings do not give very much thought to that inner craving. You simply try to cover it over with worldly experiences, with physical satisfactions. And the state of the world is such that many have even forgotten that it exists. And yet, the New Age energies (as you like to call them) are now fanning that flame within the heart of each one of you. There are dissatisfactions arising. There is confusion arising, as beings are once again brought face to face with the need to know Truth, to be in that unconditional love, to be merged with that Ocean of Love. The flame is within you. It is what has directed you on your spiritual path. It is what I am at present activating. For only when that becomes the overruling passion in your life will you have the necessary energetic empowerment to break through those final veils that keep you in the illusion of separation. Without a strong longing in your heart to be one, to know Truth, to feel that love, it is impossible to break through.

At times you recognize the presence of the inner flame as a blessing. At other times it feels like something you wish would go away, because it distracts you from your illusions, it distracts you from experiencing your individual ego self and fulfilling that life only. In a sense it causes you discomfort. But it is a divine discomfort. It is a divine longing. Within you is that divine child that wants reunion. It is not satisfied with spiritual ideology and philosophies about how we are all one with God. It is not satisfied with psychic phenomena, or the many experiences along the path that are not complete. It is only satisfied when that feeling of Union occurs, in those moments of real Oneness. Our goal is simple. In fact, it is so simple it can be accomplished, if you are ready, in one moment. To reconnect you practically in the experience of God-Realization is rather simple. It is the preparation to reach that point that can be troublesome, that takes some time. But through it all, if you can connect within the center of your being with your spiritual heart, with that divine longing that is not satisfied merely with a few channeling sessions a month, or even with a few hours of meditation per day — if you can connect with that part of you that will only be satisfied by complete Union, we will have accomplished much, and you will be ready for that final slender thread of illusion to be severed.

There is a Sufi example that illustrates a point about the importance of God-Realization, that it is indeed the entire purpose of existence. Imagine you are the servant or minister of a king, and the king has sent you on a mission into a foreign land, specifically requesting that you fulfill one particular activity, one particular act while you are in that foreign land. So you embark in your sailing vessel and go to that strange land, where you are surrounded by all of the phenomena, all the uniqueness and cultural diversity of a new kingdom. While you are there, you experience many wonders and gather many stories to relate to those in your home. And yet, somehow you neglected to remember that one simple action that your king had requested of you, the one reason that he sent you there in the first place. And then, after your time is up and you have returned and are again before your king, he says "So, how did it go?" And you say, "I experienced so much!" And you begin to recount your stories and all the wonders you witnessed and to thank the king for sending you on such an incredible adventure. And then the king says, "Well, what about that little request that I made? What about that purpose that I sent you there for?" And then you finally remember that this was the most important thing, and the one thing that you forgot. And in forgetting that, all of the experiences, all of the wonderful stories are as nothing, are just like dreams, meaningless dreams.

And so it is for human beings. To live in this world is to experience all of the wonders, all the wonderful dreams. Truly, they are here. Truly, you can enjoy them. And yet, if you do not fulfill your ultimate essential task, the purpose of your life, when you leave this world you will return to the king and all of your dreams will be just that. Perhaps you will have learned something or other. Perhaps you will have made small progress. But you will not have completed the mission. You will not reap the rewards of Union, of God-Realization, of liberation from the rounds of birth and death. On this world, human beings have continually gotten sidetracked. They are given countless opportunities, countless lifetimes, and in each lifetime the purpose is the same. And in each lifetime perhaps they get a little bit closer. But very, very few have the clarity, have the remembrance of their true mission and fulfill that.

This course is about that true mission. It is about the essential and most important thing in your life, your reunion with God, with the Source. At this time it is easier than it has ever been. There will be many, many blessings and you have already experienced some of them. If you are one who prefers to think of yourself as being on the Ascension Path, that is fine with me. I highly recommend it. And yet, beings who will experience Ascension must first experience Self-Realization. Upon experiencing Self-Realization you are in total surrender, total Union. It doesn't matter to you anymore what dimension your body is inhabiting, because you are one with all. In effect, you are already home. You are already united with that which the Ascended Masters who are speaking to you through this channel are united with. Then it is only important to you what your mission is, and when that mission is completed you will be given the opportunity to experience Ascension. This is how it has worked always on this Earth. Those beings of the Great White Brotherhood whom you enjoy communing with are beings who attained Self-Realization, completed their work here, and took advantage of the opportunity for Ascension when it was offered to them. This is, indeed, how it has always worked on Earth. And these are the guiding principles that you are working under — unless, of course, it should become necessary for some reason to evacuate the Lightworkers. This can be accomplished, but as of this moment it is not necessary or in the best interest of this world. You have work to do here and I ask you to get on with that.

Praty has guided you to ask what you will do for me. I would like to add that whatever it is you feel you would like to do for me, perhaps you could first consider what it is I would like you to do for me, and make this your priority. What I would like you to do for me is to *go beyond the mundane fascinations of the spiritual path, the tricks and the traps of the psychic realm, into the experience of Union.* You can call this experience Enlightenment, or Self-Realization, or whatever you wish. Just know that in all of the scriptures you have read, all of the historical persons that you admire so, you admire them because they accomplished this. And now we offer it to you. You have only to open to receive. You will be guided. We have created quite a team here. A team that exists both in physical form and in the higher dimensions, so that you can receive the maximum assistance possible. And I ask you to take advantage of it. I ask you to open your eyes to what is occurring now on this Earth. The transformation is taking place. The inner door is open. You have only to walk through it.

So, connect with that longing, with that inner flame within you, and let that guide you. It will pull you as it has pulled you to this meeting. It will guide you through your apparent difficulties on the path, which ultimately are nothing in comparison to the rewards. For the sincere of heart, there is surely no escape. You are all in the lifeboats. You can just relax. Feel what you are feeling, connect with that devotional longing within your heart and have no fear that you will not complete the path. Have no fear that you are unworthy, that it will be too difficult for you. For indeed, you are each unique aspects of the Godhead. You are all perfect examples, and we need you all. So, I thank you for your attendance here today. I look forward to the rest of our gatherings. I offer myself to you. Take advantage of the opportunity. I love you all so much. Good day.

THE PROCESS OF
SELF-MASTERY

Saint Germain

*G*reetings. This is Saint Germain here with you. I see you have brought your obstacles with you today. The channel has brought his also. Nevertheless, I shall do my best to dissolve them and to blast through to be with you, for this is what is highest wisdom in this moment. You see, together you have manifested this opportunity. You have created, by your intention to grow spiritually, this opportunity, this class that you are engaged in. And we have assisted, of course, to focus our energies in response to your needs. For truly you have many needs. We hear about them all the time. It is our service, our pleasure, and an honor to respond to those needs. Together we are creating an energetic that is making a difference here on this troubled planet, and especially in the lives of individual seekers, of those who are seeking the completion of the spiritual path.

You are seeking not only to enter into the spiritual path and the processes involved, but you wish to go beyond, into the experience of God-Realization and ultimately into the experience of Ascension. And you have recognized in order to get into that awareness, into that consciousness, into that more refined state of awareness and being, there are necessary steps to take. There are processes to undergo and clearings to undertake. In these processes you are always assisted. There is an Ocean of Love that surrounds you in each moment, and there are subtle pathways, subtle energetic links between your human heart and that Ocean of Love. When those connections are clear and open you feel the bliss, you feel the satisfaction, the knowingness, the Oneness. When there is obstruction within that energetic pathway, you feel separation. You feel perhaps that you are processing or clearing something; you have a sense of separation.

The process we are outlining this day involves just that, the inner journey to freedom, to liberation, to the state of Oneness. That is the essential completion you are longing for. Until that completion is attained in the Self-Realization experience, there will be feelings of separation, feelings of heaviness, or whatever emotions or energetic feelings you have. Because you see, the fact that you have entered the path, the fact that you have made that intention in your heart known to Spirit, to your teachers and guides, is what allows the clearing to truly begin. And when that clearing begins, it is as if you have taken a broom and swept in a dusty room. Clouds of dust arise. The very act of your longing to be one with Spirit has initiated these processes that you are doing your best to escape from! For they are part of the path.

It is a twofold situation, you could say. You are in the process of releasing energies that have accumulated through your karmic tendencies in all of your previous incarnations, and in this one. We are assisting you in the release of these old patterns, these old energies that cling to your emotional bodies, affecting your belief systems. The second part of the process involves Self-Mastery, involves learning to live in a way that you are no longer creating these limitations and obstacles. And as you are learning to live in this way, simultaneously you are clearing and releasing those old patterns. So there is much occurring within you. Your responsibility is to achieve mastery over those limiting tendencies and patterns and habits that have created what you are still carrying around with you, so you do not continue to create those. That is why you are given teachings, guidelines, spiritual practices: to help you to diffuse that inertia, the inertia that has created the illusion of separation within your consciousness.

There is a feeling among many Lightworkers that once they begin to perform their meditations and their spiritual practices, they should be there. They feel that if they are doing it right, there should no longer be the experience of processing all of those old emotions. But spiritual growth is a path that requires you to assume full responsibility for all that exists within you. Even if you didn't create one more negative experience in your life, you would still have to assume responsibility for the releasing of the older ones. From your limited perspective, it is all but impossible to know the reasons for all of those energies that you hold within you. At times you have glimpses of the past, and you may receive an insight that assists you in the releasing of that particular issue or energy. Other times you do not; you will just feel the process of those old energetic patterns passing through your physical body.

Really, the spiritual path comes down to learning to allow, learning to receive what you are receiving in each moment, and offering that up in a continuous motion of surrender to Spirit. As those thoughts, or feelings, or emotions come into your physical and emotional bodies, it is simply a matter of allowing them to flow through. On this path, there are essentially only two activities that you are ever engaged in. One is acceptance, the other is resistance. These experiences take many forms, but they can be broken down into these two very simple categories. When there is resistance, you feel caught up, enmeshed, surrounded, overwhelmed, because you are doing your best to push away those energies that you have held within you, trying to avoid experiencing them. Perhaps you have a judgment that they are not spiritual.

It is a process of learning to open completely and allow completely. We also have referred to this act of allowing as Surrender. The mind has its own ideas about what it would like in each moment, and about what is appropriate on the spiritual path. But your Higher Self has its own agenda, because you have asked your higher Selves to come in, to take control of your lives, to take you into the God-Realized state as quickly as possible. Come now, at one time or another, all of you have asked this. Maybe you want to be let out of the bargain: "I didn't really know what I was asking for! I should have asked only for the bliss." You can experience a great deal of bliss, a great deal of love and light, and still not complete your path. But because you have requested this in your hearts, because it is your mission here, and because time is of the essence, you are being pressed ever forward on your path. Those old energies that are still within you are being released. Today we will be working to assist you.

For, as I have said, your only activity is either resistance or acceptance. The rest is up to your guidance, up to your Higher

Self, up to God. And so, your effort in this area is very minimal. It is merely to allow yourself to undergo the process. In fact, you can't escape it, so you may as well allow it. Your resistance can only postpone it, can only draw it out a bit. You have all experienced these energies. You all know what I am speaking of.

And then there are those moments where you are surrendered, and life is just flowing through your heart, just flowing through. You are in a state where there is no strong desire for any particular manifestation or experience. You are just watching, witnessing the unfoldment. There is peace. There is contentment and love. There is the knowing that everything is unfolding just as it should, that you are making the most rapid progress you can into Union, into completion.

When you are in this state, you can actually experience the Grace that is always flowing. By relaxing yourselves, relaxing your grip a bit, by letting go of your own control, you are allowing that Grace to enter your life and sweep away limitation. There are more than enough angels, Ascended Masters, and spiritual guides to assist this process in each human being on this planet. Very few have taken advantage of the opportunity that is being offered now. When you are feeling the resistance, there is a sense, a longing within you to control your experience. You are judging it, saying, "This isn't what I want. I would rather have that. I would rather have something else." Perhaps you are feeling you would rather have anything else but what you are getting now. At times it is like this. Welcome to the spiritual path! This is not an indication that you are doing something wrong. It is an indication that you are making rapid progress and blasting through obstacles. If you were always in a state of bliss, you would perhaps feel at a certain level more satisfied, but you would be making much slower progress to your goal.

You are loved so much. Through the love that we have for you, the love that Spirit has for you, we are doing all we can to break through those veils. And you are feeling the Grace. You will feel it more and more. It will become more and more an inner sense, an inner awareness that does not leave you. You will feel a sense of bliss within your beings as you complete the release of these old energies. As you come closer and closer to that moment of Union, the bliss begins to take over. The resistance becomes a memory. You can't even remember what you were resisting, because it all becomes God. You see that you were wrestling with God, and you thought you had a chance for a while there. Perhaps He was having a conversation with someone, not applying Himself fully to overcoming your ego resistance. But in the perfect moment, He focuses His energy and you are thrown to the floor. You are in surrender. And in that moment of surrender, you recognize the Oneness. All of your control issues become totally humorous. For you see you were trying to control and receive only certain aspects of God, when in effect you could have received with equanimity each experience that was presented to you and enjoyed it all.

So I encourage you to make use of the Grace that is flowing, to take advantage of the opportunities that you have. For there are many beings who will assist you in this process. There are invisible teachers, such as myself, whom you may call upon for assistance. There are physical Masters who can assist in releasing these old marks upon your beings. There are many technologies you are aware of, meditations, affirmations, therapies of all kinds. They are created for a purpose. And in the moment you feel the need, you can open to receive the guidance toward what it is that can assist you in releasing.

So, dear ones, practice your acceptance. Practice offering up all your experiences to the Higher Self, to God. Live from trust. Don't be afraid to take advantage of the opportunities that present themselves to you. Where there is a need, there is automatically the potential for resolution of that need. Don't be afraid to experiment, to seek assistance in those times when you do feel at a loss. For there is Grace. And for you, dear ones, there is an incredible opportunity. We are working to assist in clearing as best we can. We can clear old energies, if you are willing to surrender and release them, and this can occur quite magically and spontaneously. If there is still something you need to learn within a process, you will continue to experience that process until you learn what you need to learn. The reason you are learning it is so that you can teach it to others, so that you can complete your Earth missions here.

So there is another that would like to speak with you. I would like to suggest that in the intervening time, while we are making the adjustment within the channel, you can sit and feel the presence I will bring through: the energies of the Violet Flame. Call upon the Violet Flame in your meditation practice. It is a transmuting energy of Grace that you have at your command. Thank you, my dear ones. I love you all. Good day.

FORGIVENESS

Archangel Michael

*H*ello, dear ones. This is Archangel Michael. I wish to speak with you for a few moments, and more importantly, I wish to work with you energetically. In this class we are bringing to the surface energies that need to be cleared. I am here to do the job for you. I would like to speak about liberation and forgiveness. While I am speaking, you may feel my presence and the energies of Saint Germain or the other teachers surrounding you. If you will only remain in a state of acceptance, we can accomplish much healing. It does not serve only to speak about that which is limiting you. You can do that anywhere. It serves you also to be liberated from it. This is where we come in. This is where the Grace comes in. We each work in our own ways, but in perfect harmony with one another, for your benefit.

The energies that you hold — let us call them the old negative energies that are destined to be transmuted — must be offered up. In order for you to offer up these old energies, you must be free of your attachment to them, or at least be willing to be free of attachment. One vital tool that you can utilize is the power of forgiveness. You have all judged yourselves in this and other lifetimes. You have judged yourselves harshly at times. You have judged others. You have held grudges. You have been wronged. You have wronged others, and judged yourself for doing so. Until you can utterly forgive all those who have caused you pain, until you can utterly forgive yourself for whatever transgressions, real or imagined, you will not be able to let go of those old, limiting energies that you hold. It is the act of forgiveness that separates those energies and allows them to be transmuted. It is a relaxing in the heart, in the mind, in the consciousness, of your grip on these energies and of your belief in the reality of them. Your belief that you were a separate entity in the first place, that could be harmed by another separate entity, is completely illusory, for there is only one entity. There is a burden that you can carry, and all of you do so to a certain extent. You are carrying a large or a small sack on your shoulders. It is full of old grievances and grudges and hurts, and all of these are marks on your soul that need to be cleared. In order for them to be cleared, you must have an attitude of forgiveness. Consciously forgive, and especially forgive yourselves. For through forgiveness, you arrive at the belief in your own worthiness to receive. If you have issues of unworthiness, you will not be able to open fully to receive your birthright.

The Self-Realization experience that you are longing for is your birthright. It is not something that you need to work for, earn, struggle for, and one day tip the scales in your favor so you can attain true Realization. It is something that you were meant to have all along. But on this particular planet, beings lost sight of that. Because beings lost sight of that, the spiritual path was created to bring back that awareness of Union. So just by the very act of your being, you deserve it. In fact, it is your destiny to be in that state of Union. All the illusions you hold within you that keep you in the awareness of separation are not real, are not justified by any divine law. It is only the laws that you created in your consciousness, only the laws and rules that you have applied to yourselves, that keep you feeling that you perhaps have more work to do before you deserve the blessings. But if you can forgive yourself (ultimately knowing that there is nothing to forgive) and forgive others (ultimately knowing there is nothing to forgive), you will feel your attachments, your connections to those old illusions being severed. You will feel those old energies just floating away. You will feel yourself rising to a higher frequency where those energies cannot exist. This is your process: just relaxing, releasing in whatever way works for you, in whatever moment you find yourself in. So practice forgiveness, dear ones, each day in your lives, especially towards yourselves, and also toward others. Send love, rather than vengeance, toward those who have caused you discomfort. Thank them for being your teachers in that moment, for bringing to your awareness an energy that you have yet to release.

There is no thought that is of any higher value than any other. There is no belief that is of any other higher value than another. They are all equal. They are all part of the illusory landscape. I ask you to rise above, to allow yourselves to simply float upward. Let your frequency be raised. Be willing to let go of that which you have clung to for security, your own personality complexes. It is difficult to let go of them at times, your habit patterns, your karmic tendencies, your inertia. Yet everything in your lives at this time is focusing, is at play to liberate you. All of the processes you undergo are working to liberate you. Liberation is at hand. Liberation is achieved only through Union, only when there is no possible way to believe in separation, when there is only Oneness. And I am here to assist you. I have the angelic technologies to assist you, to sever those attachments to the places where you feel stuck. You must only be willing to rise. You must only be in the state of acceptance, of surrender to the process. Let go of your control of it. It is proceeding at its own pace. You will succeed. You will achieve the liberation that you seek. Call upon me when you feel stuck, and then just allow. Call upon Archangel Michael, call upon Saint Germain, and all of your teachers, physical or non-physical ... whoever comes to mind. There is assistance for you. This class was created just for this assistance. The effects of this class are not only for these two hours when we gather together. They are ongoing. The process continues when you leave. It is occurring before you arrive. It will continue. So just offer yourselves. Know that you are loved. Just relax and enjoy, as best you can, this divine operation that is taking place.

So, I thank you for your attention. Time for me to say farewell. I will remain energetically with you throughout the rest of this class, throughout the rest of this day. I love you all so much. Good day.

GROUNDING SPIRIT IN THE PHYSICAL

Ashtar

*G*ood day. This is Ashtar here with you, back by popular demand! It is indeed a pleasure to be with you, my fellow Lightworkers, you who are fulfilling your roles in the divine play just as we in our capacity perform our parts in the play. Neither one or the other is more important, or more profound a healing for this planet. Just relax yourselves and be comfortable. I would like to speak with you for a few moments briefly and then introduce another honored guest. As I speak with you, I would just ask you to open yourselves to allow the energy of Spirit, of the divine Higher Self, to enter you and fill you and ground you. Let the energies come fully into your bodies, all the way down into your legs. Just be with us. Be with your Self and be with us, we who are here ministering to you, helping you to make this transformation more gracefully and more effectively. This is the purpose of our channeling.

So, the purpose of this holy gathering, this segment of this course that has been so thoughtfully and divinely prepared for you, is to assist you in grounding Spirit more fully into your physical form. This is a necessary process, a vital part of the preparation for those wishing to achieve the Ascension in this lifetime. You could say the Ascension is the merging of the physical and the spiritual Self. In order for you to accomplish this, it is necessary for you to allow your spiritual Self to fully merge, fully integrate, with your physical self. Rather than viewing it as a process of escaping from the physical, perhaps you could view it as a process of fully bringing Spirit down into the physical, spiritualizing and transforming that level of your being. This is what we will be helping to accomplish today.

You see dear ones, it is necessary for you to be fully present here on the Earth plane in order to fulfill your part in this divine transformation that is occurring. Many of you encounter the information about our presence, about the possibility of evacuation from the Earth. You encounter the information about the Ascension experience, and at least a few of you have perhaps felt a bit impatient for this to take place. You know who you are! It is a human reaction to this wonderful information. Perhaps you are wondering why it has not yet occurred for you. Perhaps you see no reason. I have some reasons for you today. I will try to explain it one more time for you while I am working with you energetically.

In order to heal and transform the physical Earth, it is necessary for beings in physical form to be the vital links between the dimensions, between Spirit and matter. You are acting as those links. As you ground the spiritual into the physical, you are healing the planet. You are setting up an energetic which is necessary and vital for those beings of this Earth who are destined to make the Ascension experience a reality. Some of you have asked "Why can I not immediately ascend then return and continue my work?" I will try to explain this to you also. Once the Ascension occurs, you are no longer a physical being. That link is broken. You become a higher-dimensional form. Even an Ascended Master who returns for specific purposes, manifesting an apparently physical body on the Earth plane, is not a physical being. He is a higher-dimensional being manifesting a holographic presence in the third dimension. This is not the same as you being here and bringing that spiritual presence down into your physical self. The vital link that you are is critical. As I said at the onset, the role that I play, the role that the Ascended Masters play in this drama, is no more important than the role that you are playing. We are fulfilling our service. You are fulfilling your service in being here. And it is highest wisdom and necessary for you to connect, to make the linkage, to bring the Grace that we channel to you through, all the way into your physical form and into the Earth. In doing so, this activates the other physical entities and the Earth herself. If you do not complete this grounding of your spiritual Self, you are not entirely fulfilling your mission. It is necessary, in order to complete both your service here and your Ascension experience, to fully integrate Spirit, to attain that state of Union and thus to bring it through for humanity.

So, in a sense you could say you are performing a vital function that no other beings can perform. One of the functions of this class today will be to assist you practically in completing this integration that is so vital. So you could say that the most direct path to your Ascension is to come fully into the physical experience and bring your Spirit down fully. It is not an escape. It is a matter of being present, of fully anchoring and allowing that energy to flow through to beautifully manifest here on Earth where it is needed the most. As time goes by, if you are not fully understanding my words today, you will. As time goes by, you will understand the perfection that is at play, here in this wondrous Divine Plan that neither you nor I created. We can only appreciate and serve. In doing so, there is joy. There is bliss. There is love.

As you release your limitations, your dense energies, you will find Spirit coming through more profoundly, more powerfully, into your body and into your consciousness. You will realize who you are, what you are here to do, and you will joyfully do just that spontaneously in each moment.

I would simply like to close by saying how grateful, how honored I am to be working with you on this sacred mission which is successfully concluding. There is much yet to transform, yet I can foresee the success and the completion. Have no doubt about who you are, about the reality of the Command and the Ascended Masters. Have no doubts. Trust that you will receive whatever you need to receive in each moment, because your sincerity places you in that beautiful place of receptivity. So I think you are ready now for the next guest. I will remain with you. Simply rest peacefully in this energy while I retire and allow the next speaker to come through. Thank you very much. Good day.

DIVINE LOVE

Krishna

*G*ood day. Welcome. This is the Master you know as Krishna, making my first appearance through this channel. A rare public appearance! My presence today is an initiation for you, representing the next step for you on your path. I will be bringing through a great deal of love and light, into the open vessels that you have become through all of the work that you have done in the past and the work the Masters have performed with you. The transformations that you have manifested demonstrate that you are ready and willing vessels for my energy.

The purpose behind working with any Master is to help you to achieve Union with your Higher Self, your own Divine Presence. We come as catalysts to this divine reaction. We stimulate the transformation, and yet are untouched by it. In your first class, Lord Sananda and Mother Mary spoke to you about devotional love and the longing in your heart, and stimulated that longing to a greater extent that it might assist in propelling you through this transformation. In your last class, you dealt with the transmutation of negative energies and tendencies. In this class, we will be filling you up with Divine Love and helping you to bring that love fully in, as Ashtar was suggesting. Many of you live in the mental realms. Many of you tend to live in the higher chakras. I will be stimulating the opening of the heart center. Ashtar opened you up, and I am here to assist in filling you with that premium grade energy. You learn by experiencing what it is that you need to know. Only by experiencing Divine Love fully within your forms can you truly understand what we are trying to accomplish. So beyond the words, this is my function this day.

Where there is resistance in your beings, it is often the case that you are resisting the full manifestation of your divinity in the physical. Oftentimes you feel comfortable holding Spirit at arm's length, keeping it in the mental realms or the psychic realms.

And indeed, while there is still the identification with the ego self, it can feel as if the spiritual Self is an alien intruder. "What is this energy coming into my being?" says the ego mind. It is you, your divine Self enhanced by our presence. And yet, at first it creates a bit of a dichotomy. At first there is still the clinging to the limited ego-perspective which can never fully integrate or understand the depth and the power of the Self.

As you experience the spiritual path, the divine Higher Self begins to take a stronger and stronger role in your identity, in your experience of life, until ultimately it becomes everything you are. It dissolves the limited ego-perspective entirely, until there is only the oneness of Union, of Self-Realization. You are now in the process of experiencing this dichotomy to a greater or lesser extent in your lives, and until that Union is complete, you will still perhaps see Spirit as something external coming down into you. When Union occurs, there is only Spirit manifesting in every dimension, there is only Oneness. There is never the sense of "The Other" coming in to take over or to teach. There are always new waves of energy and Grace, and the presence of various Masters to assist, but the identification with the limited ego-self is gone. This is the essential state of awareness that we are trying to teach you about in this course. As we are talking about it, we are doing our best to help you to experience it. And we will also give you some keys to spiritual practice that will help you with the completion of this Self-Realization path.

Divine Love is the essence of all. It is what you are. It is *who* you are. It is everything you can witness. It is everything you can imagine. Divine Love is the essence, the heart of the creation. For you, it is vital to learn to live in that heart. The heart space that is within your physical form is a channel, directly connecting you with the essential Divine Love energy of all of Creation, with the heart of the creative Godhead Itself. As you bring Spirit into the physical, you will find that the heart is your center and the place you live from. It is the place you can operate from most effectively here in physical form on this transforming planet. Until you can bring that compassionate Divine Love into play, or shall I say *allow* it to come into play, you will not be complete; you will not be as effective a Lightworker. As the denser energies are removed and transmuted from your being, as you learn to ground Spirit into the physical, all of your spiritual centers, your chakras, will be aligned and balanced. You will find the heart center to be that which balances all. And your spirit, your divine Self, can anchor within that heart center and fill you with a great deal more Presence, a great deal more of your own divinity, than if you were to only keep it in the mind or in the psychic centers. Bringing it down into the heart, you see, ends the feeling of separation.

You could look at it in comparison to the physical heart. The physical heart pumps the blood and the fluids through your body, oxygenating, healing, giving every cell its nurturing. The spiritual heart center pumps the love through every cell of your being and overflows your physical body, surrounding you with an aura that can be felt by all sensitive beings and that affects all beings throughout this world.

You could say it is a major aspect of your work here, to open your hearts, to allow this opening to take place and to learn to live in that center. Learn to allow Spirit to flow fully through your being, balancing and opening all your chakras, but residing in the heart. Let the heart be your organ of perception rather than the mind! Let the heart be your guide rather than the head! The mind's function is vital and necessary, but it has not the discernment of the heart.

As your resistance to Spirit is transmuted, you will find this beautiful energy of Love filling your breast, filling your being. You will find the source of bliss within your own being, and you will be able to more and more profoundly connect with that and channel it through. It ends your separation. It ends your sensation of aloneness. Perhaps you have felt deserted here on this alien planet, and you want to go home. Perhaps you are thinking that home is some other planet in some other star system. Perhaps you had incarnations there before you came here. And yet, while you were there, and while you are here, your home is always within you. It is never an external place. It is always in Spirit, in that inter-dimensional doorway that exists as your heart center. You can walk through at any time and be home. When you attain Enlightenment, Self-Realization, you will know this practically and permanently. Until that time, you will experience it more sporadically. And yet it can become your focus, your true zexperience, your true identity more and more as you allow the process to unfold.

So I would like to share with you a very simple meditation technique that will assist you in anchoring this Divine Love energy from the Self into the physical. It will assist you in your empowerment, in your release of any remaining ego attachments. You see, you have to replace the satisfaction that you gain from ego attachments with something else. You can't give up what you have and receive nothing. You must give up what you have held of limitation and receive that which is greater. So I will teach you this very simple technique. It is based upon the essential breath meditation that you have been instructed in many times. I will put a new spin on it for you.

I would like you to relax and take some deep breaths. Just relax your bodies. Feel Spirit completely within every cell of your being, just as it is. Just relax into that space. With each breath, I wish you to visualize — in your heart center — beautiful glowing embers, like the embers from a fire, burning with Divine Light. With every breath you take, feel the air entering your heart center, fanning those embers, and with each breath, visualize them growing brighter and brighter. As you breathe, you can feel your heart center radiating more and more brightly, its energy filling your entire body, shining out all around you — a three hundred and sixty degree circle — with a beautiful radiant love. If your mind wanders, just bring it back to the breath and to the heart center. Let this Divine Love energy wash over you, around you, and through you. Let it enter every cell. Let it fill every part of you with light, a nurturing and healing light. This light is gentle, yet penetrating, transmuting all fear, anger, and resistance.

Very good, my dear ones. You are all shining brightly! I wish to encourage you in the use of this very simple technique. It is something you can do throughout your day, in moments of stillness — to replenish your spiritual energies, to clear your space, to clear your energy centers. It also serves wonderfully to bring the spiritual Presence fully in.

Wonderful! I also would like to honor you for your commitment, dear ones, in attending this course and in your spiritual practice. Your commitment to being here on Earth at this time, sharing of yourselves, creates a wondrous light. It creates a healing. It gives hope to a planet that not so long ago seemed utterly hopeless. You do not know, nor can you know yet, the effects that you have through your spiritual practice. Only know without a doubt that it is highest wisdom for you to be here, to serve in this way. Bring Spirit fully into your bodies. Attain that Oneness. Reach your destination, which is your true home in the Divine Love that you are, that we all are, that we play and sing and dance within. So, my dear ones, it has been an honor to be with you. This is the first time I have channeled my presence through this particular being. And very rarely have I participated in channeling at all. So I thank you for this opportunity. Lord Sananda is the host of this course, and upon his request I have made the journey to be with you. I hope I have this opportunity again, as it is quite unique and quite beautiful. Again, I love you all so much. You are doing beautifully, each and every one. Good day.

THE PHILOSOPHER'S STONE

Serapis Bey

*W*elcome. This is Serapis here with you, slowly bringing my energies through this body form so that I can speak to you: subtly, yet powerfully melting away those few areas of resistance. Today I would like to speak with you briefly, and then another will come through. I would like to bring through the energies of Truth. As you have been discussing, love without Truth is incomplete. And likewise, Truth without love is also incomplete.

You are here on this world specifically for the purposes of personal growth and service. An aspect of this service is to be, as best you can, a beacon of Truth. For the Truth is a very powerful energy. The Truth is an energy that activates and awakens a sleeping consciousness to the awareness that there is something more, that there is a purpose in existence. This is a very important function. Without purpose, all beings would be running around in circles, experiencing life with no direction. But with purpose comes understanding. With purpose comes the sense of satisfaction, of fulfillment, and the ability to withstand the moment to moment challenges and discomforts of physical life. When you know you are here for a higher purpose, it becomes much easier to withstand the processes involved in being here. And indeed, these processes are vital to your growth. So just relax with me, and as I speak I will bring through some healing energies for you.

To use an example from the world of alchemy, Truth can be compared to the concept of the Philosopher's Stone. In ancient times, certain practices of alchemy involved the transformation of matter into different forms. One aspect, considered by the uninitiated to be the ultimate trick of the alchemist, was the ability to turn lead into gold. And in those times, there was rumored to be a substance called the Philosopher's Stone which, when touched or rubbed against lead, could transform it into gold. Really, there was no such substance. It was a device. For the true alchemists were Masters who could turn lead into gold or into anything else because they had attained that level of Mastery. And those who came after, looking for the Philosopher's Stone, looking for the proper incantation, looking for the alchemical formula to turn lead into gold, were always failures.

So you could say that you are undergoing an alchemical reaction, one which is turning the lead of your mundane consciousness into the gold of God-Realization. And in this alchemical reaction, the Truth — the vibration of Truth — is the Philosopher's Stone. For this vibration of Truth is what touches you within, initiating that reaction. It begins the reaction, supports the reaction, and completes it, always with love. And though this reaction cannot be accomplished without love, it also cannot be accomplished without the vibration and the awareness of Truth.

When I speak about Truth, please do not confuse this with merely intellectual facts. Truth is foundational, essential, unchanging. The Truth itself is that vibration, is that essential energy that is the Self, that is God, that is Spirit, that is the creative essence of all. In effect, Truth cannot be spoken in language, but can only be experienced by a human being through application of spiritual law. You must become acquainted with Truth. You must come face to face with it and accept it into your lives. You must have a relationship with that Truth. Not a relationship that you would call a flirting relationship, but a committed relationship.

What is it you say in your lives? You say, "I am flirting with the idea of this or that. I am flirting with the idea." There are many beings — the majority of beings on this planet — who are busying themselves, flirting with ideas. And there are many who are now beginning their spiritual journey, and yet still only flirting with ideas of spirituality. Perhaps you could say that you begin by flirting with the Truth, until it seduces you! And then it becomes a matter of living in that state of openness, of always wanting to know "What is the Truth? What is the highest wisdom? How can

I know the Truth that is beyond all the ideas of spirituality? How can I feel the Truth that is beyond all the ideas, that is the experience of Love itself?"

Your spiritual practice, as you are all aware by now, takes you into direct face to face interaction with the mirror of Truth. In that mirror you see yourself. You see that part of you which is real, and you see that part of you which is illusion. You see the part of you which is a figment, the ego identity, and that takes courage, doesn't it? For the Truth shakes you. It wakes you and breaks you of your attachments to the dream. It shows you that there is no satisfaction in that dream any longer. And you gradually learn to love and respect and depend upon that energy of Truth that flows direct from Source through your heart. You learn to long for that, because you know that where the Truth is, there is the Love, there is the door that leads you home. To live in the Real is simply to be in absolute respect of the Truth, in surrender to the Truth above all. And when you have choices to make, you look into the mirror of Truth before you make your choices. You have the courage to choose the highest path, though it may seem more difficult at times, because you know there is no other way if you wish to get home to that Self that is the Love, the endless and the boundless Love that can never be taken from you because it *is* you.

In our talks, our little channeled discourses, you will notice that many Masters have come through to share our specific energies with you. Each of us are like that Philosopher's Stone, for in interacting with your energy fields, there is a transformation for you — a healing, an expansion. This transformation is accomplished in the realms beyond speech or ideas. It is accomplished because your hearts have a respect and a longing to know Truth, and because the Truth is present. So, dear ones allow this reaction in your lives. Just witness it. When you have moments of unclarity, when you are not certain, call for my presence and the presence of the Masters. Ask for that vibration of Truth. That Truth will grant you experiences that you will utilize in the practice of discernment. For once you have experienced Truth, you have something to compare everything else with. And if it doesn't resonate with that Truth, it is more easily discarded. Until you have a full and complete experience of the ultimate essential Truth, in a real way, there is always the potential for confusion, for having difficulty in your choices and decisions. Once you have the essential essence of the Truth vibration within you, you have the Philosopher's Stone, the touchstone of Truth, and you can discern the lead from the gold.

So, my beloved alchemists, thank you for your attention. I will remain with you. I ask you to simply relax and breathe as we change Masters here for a moment. I love you all so much. You are doing so beautifully. Never doubt yourselves. Love yourselves as we do. Good day.

DISCERNMENT

Hilarion

*H*ello, dear ones. This is Hilarion here with you. How are we all doing today? It is good to be with you. It has been quite a while since I have visited in this way. I am acclimating to this physical form once again. The channel is always transforming, and each time I interact with him, it requires another adjustment. For we are all growing and changing and transforming, are we not? It is as if we were in a long passenger train, with many cars and many passengers, all being pulled to our ultimate cosmic destination. Your bodies are sitting in the third car from the rear of the train. My body is ordinarily in the fifth car from the rear of the train. So I have to walk through and come back a bit to interact with you.

We are all in our own process of transformation, and while we are in this process, we have many ideas and beliefs about the nature of that transformation. Sometimes we are closer to Truth, other times not. Sometimes you are sitting in your seat on the train meditating, feeling very good about yourself, knowing you are getting closer and closer to your ultimate destination in the Source. Other times you might fall asleep. You wake up and you find, "Hmm, the train has been moving all along. I thought I wasn't getting anywhere because I was asleep. But I'm still on the train." So have some trust, dear ones. I don't think you will jump off now, for this is the Flyer: never less than one hundred miles an hour!

I would like to add to what those who came before have said so beautifully. I would like to put my own feelings forward regarding the areas of Truth and discernment, regarding practical matters of living day-to-day in this life, having to make endless choices. It seems you are always having to make decisions about what to do and how to proceed, and wondering if your choices are correct, wondering if you are truly following what is highest wisdom for you. At times you judge yourself. At times you feel separate or confused, while at other times you feel yourself to be in complete alignment and Oneness, knowing the perfection. As Serapis has said, discernment is a matter of the heart. It is a matter of deepest conscience and feeling. It is an experience of inner knowingness, activated by the energies of Truth, the energies of Spirit coming from Source through your hearts and your beings. It is activated by your experience of Truth, the essential "stuff" of creation. Until you have a direct and practical experience of Divine Love and Truth, of that essence that you are, you can never achieve an accurate process of discernment. You need to learn to recognize that vibration of Truth as it moves through you directly in your spiritual practices. And then in your choices in the world, you compare that which is coming to you through your senses and through your mind, through your subtler vibrational feeling mechanisms, with the energy of Truth you have experienced within you. "Here I have a choice. Here I have two paths before me. Two things are being offered to me." And you take those into your heart, one at a time, and feel which resonates with that energy of Truth in the heart. And that is how you know which is highest wisdom for you in that moment. As you proceed on your path, this process becomes automatic. You don't have to think about it. It becomes a knowingness. It happens just that quickly, and then it is a matter of trusting that knowingness.

You could say that life is like a classroom. You're in the Earth school, learning what you need to learn, and you are presented with many tests. Most of the tests are "multiple choice." You have to choose A, B, C, or "none of the above." Your choices determine your experience here. Your choices reflect your beliefs. Your choices reflect your awareness of Truth. Your choices determine your future experiences just as those choices you made in the past are influencing you now. For example, at a certain point in time you were presented with a little flyer about this Ocean of Love workshop, and you had to choose yes or no — a yes or no decision, A or B. You chose A. There were others who chose B. Here we are, the A team! For my part I congratulate you on your choice. For others, perhaps it was highest wisdom for them not to choose this. And yet, I congratulate you. For you felt the resonance in your heart when you were presented with this opportunity. Something made you say, "Yes, I think I can open to that. It sounds like fun. It sounds like an adventure. It feels like something I need."

So the Truth vibration enters you through your spiritual practice. The energy of Truth creates a resonance in your hearts that is pure, that resonates at the same frequency as the divine Highest Self that you are. And then, when you are presented with opportunities and options, you bring those into your awareness, bring them into your heart, and you see if there is a resonance or a dissonance. It is that simple. At that point it is not a matter of "right or wrong," of "light or darkness," or any of the dualities. It is a matter of simply what is in resonance with you, with your path. Then you have no choice but to walk that path. And that path will take you through wonderful transformations, through fields of bliss and Grace, through experiences of intense release or difficulty. And you will have to trust your discernment through challenging times, knowing that you have chosen the most direct path for you.

How can you find your way home? How can you find your way through the maze of third- and fourth-dimensional experiences into the higher-dimensional being that you will soon become? You sort of feel your way along, don't you? "Well, this feels just a little bit better. I think I'll try this way." And it becomes very simple. It becomes automatic. Your discernment becomes fully activated within you and you just act upon that. You just let that guide your choices, always asking for assistance when you feel the need for it, and receiving that assistance.

This is why we cannot tell you what is right for you, or why we will not. Because it is part of your process to learn to discern, to choose for yourselves. For you need to always refine that ability as you move along to higher and higher levels of responsibility in your service in this world. You require higher levels of discernment in order to accomplish your service activities more perfectly.

Ultimately there is surrender, and the experience of Union, which is what this course and what this life are all about. Your presence here today, from my perspective, is a great blessing for this planet. It is a blessing for you as individual seekers and aspirants, and also for this world. And it is indeed an honor for us who are granted the opportunity to speak and to share our energies with you. So, let's just breathe for a few moments. In closing, I would like to share a healing with you. My energies are all loving and overflowing. Just spend a few moments with me in silence.

So, my dear ones, thank you for your attention, for your focus. In closing I will leave you with a little bit of a saying to remember me by. Just remember that, "Joy follows the one who follows the Truth." And live in that Truth always. Know that your troubles will be over as you surrender to that energy and allow it to take control of your lives. Following the vibration of Truth coming from your divine Highest Self is always highest wisdom for you, and that is how you will find your own unique manifestation of divinity, no matter what planet, no matter what dimension you exist upon. So follow the Truth and find that joy. I love you all. Good day.

TRUST

Kuthumi

Good afternoon. This is Kuthumi here with you. It gives me great pleasure to be with you, to be in your company. Such a joyous group! I can see you have done a great deal of work already. The blessings that have been coming forth as a result of these classes are quite magnificent to behold and experience. I think many of you are beginning to appreciate the Grace and blessings that you are receiving, and to enjoy them just as you have been enjoying yourselves this day. This gives us who are assisting the process a great deal of pleasure and joy as well.

On your path to Self-Realization, you will pass through many portals, many energetic doorways. You will receive many blessings, many gifts. You will receive the gifts and tools that you require on your path at the appropriate time, just as you require them. Your path is orchestrated, you see — from a very deep and perfect perspective, from a perspective that is far beyond what the participants on the path can be aware of and understand. You can indeed receive glimpses and experiences of the Grace and perfection that are at work, but only with the completion of the Realization experience can you in retrospect look back at each moment on your path and realize the perfection that was unfolding. Only then can you look back at those moments where you were challenged, where you may have been judging or misjudging what was occurring, and see that even that darkest hour was a great blessing, was perfectly required to take you into the next level of awareness.

One of these gifts or tools is the subject of today's class. That is trust. Trust is not something you can create alone. Nor is it something that your divine Self can force upon you. It is something that must be co-created. It is a gift that is vitally necessary, and one that requires your cooperation in receiving and creating it in your hearts, in your beings. It is something you must prepare to receive, open to receive, and utilize once you have recognized it. It is not something you can hold in your mind. It is something deeper. It is truly a gift of Grace.

On your path, you will pass through many challenges. You will be faced with difficulties. There will be many opportunities to doubt, opportunities to fear, opportunities to feel abandoned or confused. And at those times you will need to have trust. For no matter how well you have been prepared for the transformation into the Self-Realized state, no matter how many lectures or teachings you have received about it, when you are on that path, you will of necessity walk through areas of difficulty. You will walk through areas where all of your teachings and training will seem not to apply. They will seem to be of little help in those moments of deepest transformation, in those moments of pain and doubt. I'm sure you have all experienced to some degree what I have been speaking of.

Trust will carry you through those spaces. Trust will arise within your hearts, within your consciousness, as a presence, as a knowingness, as a mysterious yet undoubtable awareness. And this trust will give you the necessary detachment to surrender. When you are face to face with the dissolution of your separateness, your ego identity and all of the beliefs you have gathered about yourself, there may be only that trust. You may feel "Where are my guides now? Where is the Grace? I don't feel the presence of Sananda in my heart. I don't feel the presence of Mother Mary or my other guides." And you may have difficulty with meditation practice. You may have the feeling that you can't connect, that it is very difficult, and this may bring up fear and discomfort. It may bring up the feeling that you have taken a wrong turn on your path. Not so, for your path leads you directly through those areas. In fact, it is necessary for you to pass through the doubts and fears in order to recognize trust, in order to realize that you can depend upon it. Trust must become part of your inner nature, your essential outlook about existence and who you are. It is necessary, a necessary tool.

Again, it is not something you can create. You can think about it. You can pray for it. You can meditate and ask that it be present in your lives. But it will come only when you are ready to receive it, as a gift, just as all of the other blessings and gifts and attributes come to the true devotee in the perfect time. So in those moments, in those times when you feel challenged, know that one aspect of the divine drama that is taking place is happening in order that you might realize trust in your life. For you must learn to depend upon Spirit one hundred percent. You must learn to depend upon that divine Self more than you have depended upon the mind and the ego. Trust must be put into practice. And this world is your teacher. This world is the stage upon which the divine drama is played out in the third dimension of reality, and you must learn that the power of trust is a divine shield that you carry always. Its power is present not only in the higher dimensions, but in every dimension.

Trust is beyond belief. It is beyond hope. It is beyond your wishes. Trust is an innate knowing that you are receiving and experiencing exactly what you need in each moment. It is beyond the wishes of the mind for an easy life, for everything to go your way. In other words, you don't simply trust that everything will go just as you always planned and wanted it to, for it will not. You may believe that if you are on the spiritual path everything you wish for, everything you hope and ask for will automatically manifest, simply because you are on the spiritual path and you are being a "good" boy or girl. You might feel that you are doing it right, that you are living in the right way and everything must unfold according to what is most pleasant for you. [laughter from attendees] I see you have already gotten the joke! Trust is beyond this. You see, trust is an understanding, an awareness that you will receive always what you need, and that what you need is far more important than what you may want from a shallow ego-perspective.

In order to manifest trust in your lives, you must recognize and manifest discernment. For there is a fine line between trust and delusion. There are many people walking around in complete trust of things that are total fantasy, completely putting their faith in something that is a dream. Trust is an essential experience. It is not even reflected so much in externals. It is an innate knowingness, an awareness that everything that comes your way is for a purpose and that there are no accidents, that you are receiving the exact teachings and training that you require. Whether you are having a blissful time, whether you are having difficulty or feeling abandoned, still you can trust and know that this also is part of the path. Discernment is required to be able to discriminate between true trust and your hopes and wishes and beliefs. Hopes and wishes can be utilized as tools for manifestation, as prayers, but ultimately they must be surrendered. You may ask for what you desire, for what you feel is highest wisdom, but then you must be willing to let it go, trusting that whether you receive that or something else, that is what was highest wisdom for you.

Discernment is so important, as we discussed in our last class. It comes from experience. All of these gifts of the Spirit that we are speaking of manifest as a result of your deepening your commitment and your experience of who you are. Everything flows from that commitment to go within, into the real Self, into the Spirit, to experience it and let it transform you. Everything else happens spontaneously.

So there are times on the path when you will be required to make leaps of faith, to surrender. And in those moments it will be necessary many times for your teachers and your guides to step back, to surround you with light and protection, to leave you alone with your own divine highest Self. In those moments you will have trust and you will take those leaps. The only real purpose of channelings and teachings are to connect you with your own Self. In order to complete this connection, it is often necessary for we as your teachers and guides to step back and remove our vibrations from your energy field, to allow this Union, and to protect you while it is occurring. You could envision it as if you are standing in a circle of Masters at these times, and though you are surrounded and protected, you may feel alone. You are not alone! It is highest wisdom in that moment for you to feel alone with the

Self that you truly are, and in that moment there is the need for trust. Trust allows you to relax, to surrender. Trust must be proven time and again in the divine drama. It is shown to you over and over again so that in those critical moments of transformation into the Self-Realized state, when you are left alone with just the Self of Selves, you can trust and surrender to the divine process of unification.

So, my beloved ones, I wish to share with you how much you are loved, how much you are cared for. A being who commits to the spiritual path, who has walked through the beginning and intermediary stages and is approaching the completion of the path, is surrounded by so many angelic and ascended guides. The universe opens its doors. It honors you. For you are a precious commodity in this world, and you are treated in that way. And as you proceed on your path, ever more and more Grace and assistance are available to you out of divine Love and compassion; and because you need it! Those final steps can be the most challenging, and therefore the most Grace is there. As you learn trust, it becomes a vital part of your awareness, and you just learn to live in that state. And then whatever is occurring in the world, whether it looks positive or negative or however, it loses its power over you. For you are living more in Spirit than in illusions and beliefs. So all of the divine dramas are underway. You are all experiencing them. You are all learning to trust. You are learning what it is, learning how to co-create it, how to receive it, how to believe in it. You are learning that it is not an illusion or a delusion. You are realizing that when you are trusting Spirit you are not simply burying your head in the sand like an ostrich, but truly, you are burying your head in the breast of the Divine Mother. You are realizing that when you require guidance it will be there for you, and that you can be clear enough to receive it and act upon it. You will have moments of stillness where it is appropriate to wait. You will have moments of action where it is appropriate to act, to be in motion. And through it all you will trust. You will know that you are doing just what you need to do.

You will trust in your own inner Self, your own feelings in the depths of your heart, and that will give you the peace that you require to surrender to this wondrous transformation.

You are doing beautifully. It is extremely blissful to be in your presence, to be given the opportunity to speak. Just rest in this silence and stillness for a few moments as another Master enters this physical body. It is a complex and truly mystifying process, this channeling, yes? I love you all so much. Good day.

THE INCOMPARABLE
ENLIGHTENMENT

Buddha

*G*ood day, my dear ones. How are you doing this day? I am the one you have come to know as the Buddha. I will attempt to share my love, healing, and wisdom with you for a few moments here. I will attempt to bring through my presence in this form you call channeling. I surround you all with a vast ocean of Mercy and Bliss. Indeed, we are together in this ocean for all time, each of us fulfilling the role that we have been granted in the divine play, the ongoing play that carries us through many manifestations, many lifetimes, many dimensions, in an ever expanding spiral of consciousness. I will speak a few moments and share with you my own perspective on the Self-Realization path, the path to the Incomparable Enlightenment.

That which you seek, you already are, and you know this in your hearts. Enlightenment is both your destination and your natural, inescapable state of being. For there can only be Oneness. In reality there is no separateness. It is only the subtle belief in the separate individual identity that keeps you in the state of illusion. Upon awakening into Self-Realization, you will recognize that this belief has always been a dream. You will recognize, quite simply, that you have always been one with the Source. It is a subtle shift in consciousness. The drama unfolds in many ways. The path winds uniquely for each of you. Yet no matter where your footsteps may tread on the path, you ultimately return to the center point. You return home. You each must pass through that same divine gate into Union. On the way, it is impossible to fully know or to accurately judge your progress, your merits, your de-merits. In fact, you can throw away your lists of de-merits and merits!

You must give yourself to this path as if you were going toward a destination, until you arrive and realize you were always there. Enlightenment is like awakening from a dream. When you're dreaming in your beds, the dream is everything. When you awaken you recognize, "Oh, it was just a dream. Here I am back in my normal state again." And so it will be for you when you awaken from the dream of separation. You will find yourself back in your normal state again, almost as if you had never left it. Perhaps it will seem as if it was a long and tedious dream, but at that point it will be impossible to fall asleep again.

You see, all teachings concerning this path toward Enlightenment are only temporary remedies to a temporary malady, your temporary malady of separation. Teachings are like a boat or a raft that you use to reach a destination. At first you are on the shore of illusion. As you begin your spiritual journey, you take your teachings and lash them together and make a firm raft. You push off and paddle your way towards the other shore. With Grace and assistance and effort, you reach that shore where you achieve Enlightenment, the continuous awareness of the incomparable, all-pervasive reality that exists, that is the foundation of existence, the still center out of which all is created. You realize eternal Union with that Supreme essence. At that point, what are you going to do with those teachings? What are you going to need that raft for? You are already on the shore. You are in the Buddha Lands. So you will recognize your teachings for what they are. You will be grateful. You will cast them off and be free, having no more need of limiting concepts about spirituality or any other subject. You will be beyond semantics. You will be beyond the point where you can misunderstand. But we must indeed be practical and honor those teachings that we are receiving. For you receive the perfect teachings at the perfect time, as you have been throughout this course, throughout your lives.

The bliss of Union is truly a transcendent experience, and yet it is simultaneously quite ordinary. There continue to be shifts and changes in external situations and relationships in the world. What is unique and different is your perspective, the state from which you observe the changes occurring. No longer believing in the illusion of a separate ego identity, you are one with all. There is nothing left to defend, nothing left to protect, nothing left of your ego personality to "market."

The awakening into the transcendent state of Enlightenment occurs for each being in a unique way, and you must honor that. You must learn to live with some dispassion towards your own processes and experiences. Try to understand that the very belief that you are here is a dream. There is just a very small ego-mechanism in place that keeps you focused on this third dimension of existence. It is necessary to maintain your life focus here, your consciousness focus. Yet when that ego becomes obsolete and dissolves, only its necessary functions remain, a sufficient thread of third-dimensional personality to get you through your days, so you don't forget the social customs of the moment whatever they might be. And yet, behind that veil, behind that small infinitesimal point of ego, is an expanse of existence, an expanse of bliss, a cosmic dynamo, and you are merged with that. This expansive Self is what you are, and the ego is seen as just some sort of "front man." It no longer matters to you whether others identify you as the ego or as the true Self that you are. It no longer matters what anyone thinks.

This experience of liberation occurs always in the moment that you are in. There is no escaping that reality. When you find yourself drifting into dreams of future, dreams of the past, desires, longing for that which is not manifested in the moment, bring yourself back. Take a few breaths, and again recognize that the doorway to Enlightenment is in the present moment always. It is not something you will construct. It is something you will realize, something that has always been here. And when you realize it, you will say, "Why did it take me so long? It is so simple. It is so apparent. It is so magnificent. It is so obvious."

You will all cross that threshold, dear ones, at the perfect time for you. There are many, many Masters, many energies at play. At this prophesied time, so many potential Buddhas are arriving. There are so many now who can understand teachings that could only be understood by a few in the past. There is additional Grace. There is a divine dispensation, and many, many will attain

Liberation. So I encourage you to have faith. I encourage you to wake up. When you find yourselves enmeshed in your lives, perhaps let there be a glimmer of Truth there to remind you that you are just a dream, a dream in the universal mind. So give yourselves to your path, my dear aspirants. Call upon me for assistance in your meditations. We are available to you. We are you! When you know that, that is when the true enjoyment of life begins. I will share with you some energetic transmissions as we shift, for there is another who would like to speak now. I thank you for your attention. Good day.

BLISS

Sananda

*H*ello, my dear ones. This is Sananda here with you. I have come to share my presence with you once again, in the same way as we all have come to share our energies, our love, our bliss, our strength and courage, our sense of humor, all of which you will need in order to make that crossing. You will need these attributes and more. These attributes are gifts of Spirit to you, for your sincerity, for the energy you expend in your spiritual practice, and by the very fact of your birthright as human beings.

I would like to speak to you about bliss and surrender. What do you want first, the good news or the bad news? Actually, it's all good news. Bliss is, you could say, a reward of surrender. Bliss is the very atmosphere, the very air of Heaven. It is like the air that you breathe, always present. Sometimes it is windy and strong. Sometimes it is still and peaceful. But that bliss is at the foundation of all that exists. In order to experience it — an experience I highly recommend — you must find the Kingdom of Heaven that exists within you, for that is where you will find the bliss. Many beings have searched for this Kingdom for many lifetimes. For thousands of years, human beings have sought to create an experience of Heaven on Earth. None have achieved it. They have experienced momentary glimpses. They have attempted to create their own sheltered paradises. But very few have experienced the bliss that exists when one realizes the Source. Once you have tasted that, all worldly experiences pale in comparison. That bliss draws you ever forward, and you recognize the need for spiritual practice, the need for surrender to Spirit.

Bliss can be shared, for it is transmitted from heart to heart, from being to being. You transmit it in your daily lives when you are experiencing it. At times, you transmit it even when you are unaware. At times you receive it, apparently, from another who is experiencing it, as in our channelings. It is a very elusive experience, for when you become attached to it, it seems to vanish. And when you surrender your attachment, it seems to arise.

On Earth, you need to breathe the air, the atmosphere, in order to survive. On the spiritual path, you need to breathe the air of Heaven. You need to breathe the bliss. For that becomes your sustaining force, that which feeds you. As you begin to lose your fascination with the material world and its dramas, that which arises to take its place is that spiritual bliss. You learn to tap into it from the Source, directly through your divine Higher Self, and it becomes your sustenance and your joy, your food, and drink, and breath.

You could say that bliss is like the marketing tool of God. You may hear someone giving a spiritual discourse of some kind, speaking about the path of God-Realization, and if you can feel an emanation of bliss from that person, that will be the selling point. "Oh, I want what they're having." If we told you of all of the challenges, the aches and pains of transformation, that would not be as effective an advertisement. So, the bliss is both the true nature of that experience and that which lures you in to your utter destruction, the utter destruction of your separateness, of your belief in the reality of your individual personality. All of human life has been based upon this belief in separation. All social structures are designed to handle a population who believe that they are all separate individuals. When this begins to break down, when people recognize that they are not separate individuals and begin to live in oneness, there is a transformation that must take place in all internal and external structures. There is a divine kingdom that begins to take hold, to take root, even here on the Earth. And this will manifest in your time, and the Earth's atmosphere will become the air of Heaven.

So the work that you do, dear ones, is indeed beyond my ability to praise. Honor yourselves. Love yourselves. Accept the opportunity to breathe that blissful atmosphere and take it into your lives. Since you will have to go through the transformations, you may as well eat some of the icing as well. The icing is sweet.

In every bite of cake, there is the sweetness of the icing. So, surrendering to this moment, to that which is present in all dimensions of space and time, is your key, always. This is your key to liberation and enlightenment, and the perfect preparation for that which awaits you through all those transformations, through all dimensions: the same surrender, the same bliss, only growing and growing.

So it has been our pleasure to work with you in this course. I'm speaking for myself and for all of those who have come through. It has been very successful. It will continue to be successful. Just drop your negative feelings and attachments and love yourself. Drop your feelings of inadequacy. They are useless. They are meaningless. They are dreams. It's just a matter of letting go to that which is. We will be with you. You will receive all the teachings you require, no matter how long it takes you. We will be there to support you. Whether it occurs for you tomorrow, in years, or in lifetimes ... on this world, or any other world that you may find yourself. I am holding your hand, and I will not let go until you are home with me. Thank you so much. Good day.

OPENING TO RECEIVE

Mother Mary

*W*elcome, my dear ones. This is Mother Mary here with you on this beautiful, peaceful spring day. There is much that we have to share with you today: much grace, much healing, much love. Indeed, you are both wise and fortunate to have planted yourselves in this room at this time. Now that you have planted yourselves here, it is up to us to water you, to give you the proper fertilization and nurture you in your growth. So just relax yourselves, my tender little blossoms!

I would like to speak a bit about the need to nurture yourselves. It is vital that you learn to care for yourselves, as you are on a very steep and challenging spiritual path, processing and releasing old karma and negative energies. As you are transforming very quickly, you require a great deal of support. This support comes to you from all levels of existence. It must come, of course, from your physical and non-physical teachers, and it does. And yet, it also must come from you yourselves, out of self-love and self-acceptance. These challenges of growth are indeed perfect for each of you. It is also perfect that you take advantage of opportunities that come before you, opportunities such as this gathering, opportunities to receive healing and nurturing. For you will require much assistance to complete this Ascension path. It is not practical to merely think that you can work only with invisible teachers and receive from them all that you need. There will be times when your physical body requires healing, requires love and support and nurturing. And then you have the choice before you to accept or deny that for yourself.

Love is ultimately the healing force, the rejuvenating power. It is both what you are and what you long for, especially here on Earth, the planet of emotion and feeling, the planet of self-expression. As you open yourselves, as you all are on your spiritual path, opportunities will arise for you: opportunities for healing, opportunities for communion with Spirit. I encourage you now to be open to receive, to take advantage of these opportunities. You have here in this one room a beautiful group of beings dedicated to spiritual growth. They are dedicated to the completion of their Earth missions, to serving, to channeling their individual Spirits and other healing energies. You have around you in this moment a support group. You also have around you in this moment an invisible support group. There are many angelic beings serving each of you, as well as the Ascended Masters. For we recognize the challenge of growth at this time on this planet. And where there is need, love must enter and fill the need and perform the healing.

What we have witnessed is that oftentimes love and healing are available, but they are not accepted for some reason or other — either through feelings of unworthiness, due to your over-activity, or due to stoicism. But it is time now to be humble, to be childlike, to be honest about what it is you need in your life, to pray for that and to open to receive it. The universe and the spiritual hierarchy await your prayers and your calls. At times we cannot interfere; at other times we can help. Whatever is highest wisdom, as ordained by your divine Higher Selves, is what is allowed. For your parts, it is simply a matter of learning to open and receive what is available, of learning to follow those subtle intuitions, those subtle messages that you feel within yourselves. It is all about the care and feeding of Lightworkers, and you do have a responsibility to yourself. You are not here to sacrifice, to suffer. There is plenty of that without going out and looking for more! So I encourage you, my dear ones, my dear children, to open in every way — not merely in your meditation practices, but open your hearts to one another. Support one another on your path. Let the community be formed that creates the space, the environment and the support necessary for beings to complete the spiritual path on Earth. Know that you are not alone, either in Spirit or in this world. And many more will be coming. More will be coming to your groups, and to you as individuals, with questions, with unmet needs. And you, I suggest, can be as examples of how a being loves themself enough to accept the Grace of Self-Realization, the ultimate gift.

It is all a gift to you, even those experiences that are painful at times, even those areas where you feel stuck. They are gifts to you. And as you unwrap those gifts, you finally recognize the nature of each gift, the higher purpose that it served in your life, and why you had to receive that gift at that particular time. If you are still having problems in certain areas, you are still unwrapping the gifts. You don't always know what they are. You are just unwrapping them in each moment. And then, like children on Christmas morning, sooner or later you will find yourself sitting in a great pile of wrapping paper and ribbons, with a huge pile of presents, and then you will realize the perfection.

So know, dear ones, that each moment is a perfect unfold-ment for each of you. Just receive. Surrender to the moment. Ask for Grace and assistance. Call for help from those who are offering their services. Take care of your physical bodies, your emotional bodies, your spiritual bodies, for we love you. By doing so, we can assist you even more. You will feel our presence even more. You will feel the presence of your own divinity piercing the veils, until finally that Union is complete. So support one another. Nurture one another. When you gather together in this way, it is so beautiful. My love is with you. My heart opens to you.

So, time for me to allow another to come through. I thank you for your love and support of one another. I thank you for your attention. Your sincerity is a radiance. Your innocence, your purity of heart, are brilliant to behold. Honor yourselves. Never compare yourself with another. Only be who you are. That is your most direct ticket. So thank you for your open ears this morning, and your open hearts. Good day.

THE GATE OF THE MOMENT

Sananda

*S*o, dear ones, how are you doing this day? This is Sananda here with you, your Ascended Master of ceremonies! I come with a question for you, a rhetorical question. For after I ask it, I will ramble on for some time. The question is: "What is the greatest challenge on the spiritual path?"

The answer is: "Everyday life!" It seems the structures, foundations, and thoughtforms of this world are based on the illusion of separation from Spirit. It is an illusion. It is a dream. And yet, most of the manifestations that you encounter each day are projections based upon this illusion of separateness: the fears, the mistrust, all of the learned negative tendencies that have sprouted up so profoundly on this otherwise lovely planet. Because you are sensitive and opening, yet still existing in this world, in daily life these energies do affect you in certain ways. Not always, but much of the time. Indeed, to go and sit in a cave and meditate is a way to insulate yourself, to isolate yourself from these negative energies, but it is also isolating you from a full and complete realization of the magnificence of the divine play. For within that divine play, even those so-called negative energies have a role, have a direct and important teaching role for you. They are strengthening and empowering you. The energies of this world penetrate your emotional bodies. They "push your buttons" and bring up the energies that you need to clear in order to become more fully realized, more blissful, more connected.

It is a testament to each of you, to your courage, to your strength, that you have chosen to come here at this time, to walk this steep path of Self-Realization and Ascension in a world that is undergoing massive emotional clearing and healing. Indeed, it is quite a task you have set for yourselves, quite a challenge you have accepted. For not only is there your spiritual path, there is the grocery store, there is family life, there is your career, there is money … all of these aspects of life that must still be maintained and honored even while you are undergoing this incredible transformation. If you feel at times overwhelmed, please do not think less of yourselves. Consider all that you are doing. We honor you for your commitment, for your openness, for the strength that you have shown. Indeed, only the strong of heart were invited to this party in the first place! And not only is there your spiritual practice and your worldly lives, but there is the planetary Ascension process that is occurring in each moment. The world under your very feet is transforming. There is a quickening of energies transforming everything even more profoundly. Where in all of this is your sanctuary?

Within each moment there is a gate, and that gate opens into a state of surrender that is beyond whatever external phenomenon you are encountering, whatever your mind and body and emotions are encountering. Each moment holds this beautiful gate of surrender, and that gate opens into your sanctuary. You will find that the dreams you have held onto in the past for security, for satisfaction, do not provide you with that feeling, that security, that nurturing, that safety, that connection. You will find that your memories of the past, no matter how beautiful they may have been, do not bring up that feeling of connection and sanctuary within you, that feeling of Union. It is only the real and practical opening to the Self within you in each moment that opens the gate that allows you to cope with this life, to transform in the ways that are required in order to maintain that peace and joy. That moment, fortunately for you, never leaves. You go to the gas station. You are pumping the gasoline. You spill it on your hands. The moment and the gate are still there. In that moment you have a choice to become angry or disturbed, or to laugh at the absurdity of life and enter that open gate of surrender.

Human beings come before you with their strange projections and dreams, and your reactions to those color your experience. To hold to the Real in each moment, in each moment as it opens, is your path. That is all you have to cling to in these final stages of growth. And in that moment is the Love, is the Light, is the Grace that takes you home. It only exists now. And "now" becomes that timeless place where you can dwell, where we dwell, where all Masters dwell.

So let's say, just hypothetically, that you have bought my discussion so far, that you like my sales pitch! "Well, that gate sounds pretty cool. I think I'd like to get my hands on that and go in there. In fact, help! Help me to go in there." I will give you a beautiful technique which I have given many, that will help you to open that gate, to enter that moment, that state of surrender. That technique is simply to breathe, to meditate upon the breath in each moment no matter what your activity. The breath is the breath of the Creator flowing through all time and space, supporting, enlivening, and inspiring life. The breath is the source of inspiration.

Let's say, for example, you're driving your automobile, thinking about something your boss said to you. Maybe it was something completely unfair, misrepresenting your true feelings or true performance, something entirely unjust. Maybe you received blame for something that you were innocent of, and now you are having difficulty letting go of it. It is pushing your buttons. It is touching those places, those energies within you that still need to be released. You're still driving the car, whatever that experience is bringing up. And even then, in that very moment, breathe and offer it up. Have the courage to say to yourself, "All right, what is it that I'm supposed to be learning from this experience?" and offer it up on the breath. And when you spill the gasoline on your hands, try to see the humor in it and offer that up also. In each moment you are existing, you are breathing. That is your vital connection to Spirit in each moment you are alive. And while you are alive is the time to enjoy life. While you are alive is the time to take advantage of the opportunities. You never know how long you are going to be here. You never know how many more days you have. Each day is an opportunity to open further, to surrender yourself, to enter that gate, and to receive the bliss and the love. In any moment, you can experience death. In any moment, you can attain Union, Self-Realization.

So there is one practical technique for you: the breath meditation. Another technique, not so much a technique, more of an attitude, is a sense of humor. Just look at the absurdity of the situation. Truly, the Creator has a wonderful sense of humor. Look at your physical form sometime in the mirror from an objective standpoint, not from all of your previous training and all of the times you have looked at it before judging your hairstyle and all of your other attributes, but just go objectively and look in the mirror. What a creature! What is it? What are those liquid pools that you are looking out of? What is that bushy stuff that's on top of your head? The amazement of the senses! What a creation a human being is! The absurdity and the humor come in because a human being, and all beings, are ultimately one with the Source. All sense of a separate identity is ultimately illusory. So you are looking at a figment, something that you co-created to teach yourself something, to experience life on Earth. You don't know yet why you would have created this in this way, because you are still unwrapping the gift. Once it is unwrapped, you will be grateful for it. But you must admit some humor into your lives. Allow yourself the opportunity to be playful, to be light. Otherwise you can become so serious that you miss all the enjoyment of the spiritual path. You can miss the enjoyment that opens when that gate of the moment opens. You might miss the enjoyment of the sun on your skin, of the way the ocean air smells, of all of the miracles of life. Have an attitude of joy and acceptance, of gratitude for each moment in its unfolding. Each moment is a gift for you to unwrap.

So, my beautiful and wondrous beings, again I say to honor yourselves and, as Mother Mary has suggested, open to whatever nurturing, whatever assistance you require on this path. This path will take you through many experiences, through many transformational processes, through many experiences that are blissful and joyful beyond description. And at the completion of the Self-Realization process, you will understand that all those experiences were the same, ultimately, essentially. It is all the divine play of consciousness unfolding, and this realization will allow you to enjoy it even more. So, dear ones, give yourselves to your path. Give yourselves to your meditations. Get the assistance that is available to you. Know that it is unfolding so beautifully, so divinely. Know that you are examples of that unfoldment. So honor yourselves and love yourselves. Don't be self-critical. When you feel you have made a mistake, offer that up as well. Don't get into negative emotions of guilt. There is enough of that around without creating more. Just offer it up. Be honest. Be sincere. "Well, what am I learning in this moment? What is this apparent mistake teaching me? Some way that I can be more direct, more connected, more loving, more in service, undoubtedly."

So give thanks for all of your lessons. Your everyday life, your greatest challenge on the spiritual path, is also your greatest teacher. You will only receive the lessons that you require, and only so long as you require them. So be good learners. Don't take yourselves too seriously. Just enjoy. Just surrender. Know you are proceeding as rapidly as you can on this path, which is truly majestic in its unfoldment. I will be with you throughout this day and throughout your lives. Take advantage of my presence. Ask for assistance when you require it. I will do my utmost to share my love with you. Ultimately, we are all brothers and sisters. We are family. We have a special connection, a special love. Take advantage of that love. It is yours. Enter the gate of the moment for your safety, security, sanctuary, love ... for your spiritual food, and to find out what's truly happening in your life. That is where all of the answers are found. So let's just take perhaps two or three minutes to meditate together and I will share a bit of a healing with you in silence.

Very well. Wonderful! Wonderful exercise, dear ones. Thank you for your attention. I love you all so much. I am with you. I am with you and waiting inside the gate of the moment to take each of you in my arms, for that is the gate that leads you home. I wait to welcome you home in each moment. I love you all. Good day.

About the Author

Eric Klein

Eric Klein was initiated and began his spiritual practice in 1972. He began channeling the Ascended Masters in 1986, and between 1989 and 1997 he channeled the Masters in hundreds of public sessions for groups in California and across the U.S. and Canada. Transcriptions of some of these channelings were published as books (*The Crystal Stair; The Inner Door, Volumes I & II; Jewels on the Path;* and *Sacred Journey*). As of this printing, Eric's books have been translated and published in eight foreign languages, and the messages in these books have been spread from one person to another until they have covered the globe.

Eric lives in Santa Cruz, California with his wife Christine, who is an acupuncturist, Qi Gong teacher, and devotee of Amma Chi. He currently balances his time between his continuing spiritual practice, book and tape publishing, songwriting, and music projects.

Contact Information

To receive a catalog of Eric Klein's books and channeled tapes, write to:

> Eric Klein Tapes
> P.O. Box 498
> Santa Cruz, CA 95061-0498

or e-mail your request to eklein3030@aol.com

For information about Amma Chi, contact:

> M.A. Center
> P.O. Box 613
> San Ramon, CA 94583-0613
> Tel. (510) 537-9417
> Fax (510) 889-8585

Shawn Monroe first came to know Eric through tapes of his channelings, and then became a regular attendee at Eric's channeling sessions. After Eric saw samples of Shawn's artwork, he felt that Shawn would be a good choice to do the cover art for this book. Shawn graduated from the Academy of Art in San Francisco in 1994, and currently works for Accolade Inc. You can reach him as follows:

> Shawn Monroe
> 1205 Broadway #2A
> Santa Cruz, CA 95062
> (831) 458-0470